Things My Dog Has Taught Me

Things My Dog Has Taught Me

About being a better human

JONATHAN WITTENBERG

HODDER

First published in Great Britain in 2017 by Hodder & Stoughton
An Hachette UK company

1

This paperback edition first published in 2018

ISBN 978 1 473 66438 8
eBook ISBN 978 1 473 66439 5

Printed and bound in the UK by Clays Ltd, Elcograf S.p.A.

Hodder & Stoughton policy is to use papers that are natural,
renewable and recyclable products and made from wood grown in sustainable
forests. The logging and manufacturing processes are expected to conform
to the environmental regulations of the country of origin.

Hodder & Stoughton Ltd
Carmelite House
50 Victoria Embankment
London EC4Y 0DZ

www.hodder.co.uk

To Nicky, Mossy, Libbi and Kadya
And to Safi and Mitzpah, the dogs we've loved,

And to Eva Aperia, who adores the dogs
And Leslie Lyndon, whom both dogs adored,

And to all dogs longing for loving homes.

Also by Jonathan Wittenberg

The Silence of Dark Water: An Inner Journey
Walking with the Light: From Frankfurt to Finchley
My Dear Ones: One Family and the Final Solution

Contents

Acknowledgements

But as soon as we begin ... a large nose emerges above the side of the table, slowly edging upwards, followed by an eager mouth and unwaveringly focused eyes

This book began almost as an afterthought at a meeting with my agent Jonny Geller and my editor Andy Lyon. 'Write something short and popular,' they said, throwing up a range of subjects, anti-Semitism, love, hate, none of which appealed. 'But I could write about my dogs,' I said, half as a joke, as I was about to leave their office. 'Great idea,' they both responded, slightly to my surprise. No doubt they realised before I did that such a book would take me to many of life's great themes: faithfulness, companionship, loss. Andy and Jonny have remained constantly encouraging since.

Before starting to write, I wanted to learn more about the wide-ranging relationships between dogs and people. A key moment was when I sat down with veterinarian Marc Abraham, who founded Pup Aid. He not only gave me an extensive list of people to see, but also immediately took the trouble to make personal introductions. It was due to him that I met Peter Egan, who told me how having dogs had made him care passionately about animal welfare. It was thanks to Marc, too, that I got to know Jane Holmes and the remarkable team at Medical Detection Dogs, as well as Charlotte Leng and the staff of Canine Partners. I am grateful to them all, for their love of dogs and people, and for their astute and compassionate understanding of how we can help one another. I would also like to thank Martin Segal, Noach Braun and those who train guide dogs in the UK, Israel and across the world. I also spoke with representatives of several organisations working to prevent the cruel treatment of domestic animals, a subject on which, as a committed vegetarian, I feel very strongly.

Andy Lyon and the team at Hodder could not have been more supportive. As the book began to grow they told me frankly, but kindly, what was funny, what was not and where the tail was wagging the dog. I am grateful for their enthusiasm, trust, support and guidance.

Acknowledgements

Barbara Jackson a long-standing friend, is a wonderful artist and illustrator. I am grateful that she agreed to draw the illustrations, with customary elegance, accuracy and grace.

It was my grandmother Charlotte from whom I first learnt what the companionship of a dog could mean; I don't think she ever got over the loss of her beloved greyhound Prinz. But no puppy ever trotted across the threshold of the home in which I grew up. We were a cat family and I adored our black Persian Fluffy. For a long time, my parents thought I might become a vet.

It wasn't until Nicky and I were married that sharing our lives with a dog became a real possibility. 'I think you'd love it,' said my mother-in-law Ursula when I expressed my hesitation. She's been proved one hundred per cent right, and I am grateful to her and the Solomon family for bringing the love of animals back into my life.

Our first dog, Safi, was found by a congregant in the street: I owe Russel Thomas, his mother Sandra and her brother Leslie, my much-missed colleague, the fifteen years of happiness which that kind and faithful creature brought us. I am grateful, too, to my congregants who have appreciated, or at least tolerated, the frequency with which my dogs attend the synagogue, a habit which I hope more of them will come to emulate. It may be because of my bad example that I believe my community has more dogs per human capita than any other Jewish congregation in the world.

My loving appreciation goes first and foremost to Nicky, who understands how to look after and, most importantly, how to discipline, dogs. I am grateful for all the years we've shared first as a couple, then accompanied by our four-legged companion, and for the last almost twenty-five years as each of our three children Mossy, Libbi and Kadya has joined us on our adventures following Safi's tail across Highlands and Lowlands, through rivers, forests and fields of rapidly fleeing sheep. For the children, a dog has been a natural part of the family from the first. It was they who persuaded us that we really should take Mitzpah, our second owner, home with us from the farmyard in Wales where he was born.

My parents, too, swiftly came to love our dogs. Mitzpah knows that Isca, my mother, is the second-softest touch from whom to obtain titbits underneath the table.

The dogs have opened my eyes and heart to beauty and tenderness I would not otherwise have noticed, without being so perfect as to provide me with no moments of embarrassment which I still ponder with shame. I am grateful to dogs, to nature and to life.

Jonathan Wittenberg

Introduction

There is so much I wouldn't
have noticed without my dogs

The January sun gleams over the east Devon valley, illuminating the bare branches of the trees on the crest of the opposite hill. Seagulls traverse the air, crying in the pale blue dawn. My dog and I walk slowly up the field, breathing the sharp air of the cold new day. He pauses by the base of a wild hazel, by the mossed trunk of a wind-stunted hawthorn.

There is so much I wouldn't have noticed without my dogs. It isn't that I didn't look before; I've always loved

1

to hike and wonder. My family have been my companions, fellow adventurers across forests and hills, through bogs, moors and streams, always returning muddy, tired and happy. But without the dogs I wouldn't have been out so early on so many woodland and mountain mornings, or walked so late beneath the winter stars. I wouldn't have turned unafraid down paths too overspread with thick-leaved branches to admit the moonlight, or crossed for hours the empty moorlands with only the company of rocks and water and grass.

I wouldn't have experienced that special dimension of love which transcends the human and brings animals too within its embrace. I wouldn't have known what reaching out a trembling hand to touch the fur on a dog's back could mean to an elderly lady transported to the solitary landscape of Alzheimer's disease. I wouldn't have understood how stroking a dog's head could prove so vital a bond with life for a young man too sick and exhausted for the laborious formulation of words. I wouldn't have appreciated the comfort a dog's tongue could bring, licking away tears, transforming an anguished face from pain to consolation.

I wouldn't have watched with my children how Mitzpah, our second dog, rushes for the beach in headlong, headstrong eagerness or how, released from the lead, he spins a crazy dance in widening circles of delight, before spiralling off for the nearest bank of trees. Nor would I have observed how Safi, our first dog, who had never in his life experienced snow, refused to leave the sleeper train when it stopped at the icy platform in the Highlands until I descended first, after which he carefully placed his feet on my shoes, before testing with a single, tentative paw the unfamiliar cold, white powder.

I wouldn't have felt a companion adventurer at my side as I tried to pray, to still my mind and listen, and hear, in the touch of the wind on the grass, the breath of the life of all being. I wouldn't have understood how deeply we belong together, humans, dogs, trees: everything imbued with the gift of life by the spirit which flows through us all.

Judaism has blessings for every eventuality. When struck by the beauties and wonders of creation one says, 'Blessed be God in whose world it is thus.' I like to say under my breath in addition, 'Blessed be God, in whose world there are dogs.'

What follows are some of the attitudes and skills I have learnt from my dogs, as well as some I most certainly don't intend to adopt. Though who am I to judge? For all I know, they would consider me an inadequate pupil, inept at imitation and lacking the same capacity for undivided concentration. What I should say then is that, alongside the wisdom humans have to offer, I'm trying to learn from dogs too. Some have to teach us about the heartlessness of cruelty, of which they are so often the victim; others of the utter and total devotion of unqualified loyalty and unequivocal love.

How we gave away our hearts

*He was happily suspended . . . teeth entrenched in the
thick knotting of the rope*

I wasn't always a dog fan. On the contrary, I grew up
adoring cats. When I was nine I even led the feline
team in the class debate on whether cats or dogs made
better pets; I've grown wiser since. Today, I couldn't
imagine my life without dogs. I couldn't envision being
without the companionship of a faithful, affectionate,
mischievous hound sleeping by my feet (or on the bed),
racing ahead along the path or silently staring up at
me with that meek, accusatory gaze with which they

try to convince the world in general, and their owners in particular, that they've never eaten a proper meal or been taken for a decent walk in their entire lives.

Afterwards, when it's all over for me here on earth, if there is a hereafter I hope there will be animals there too. I agree with the man who said, 'If there aren't any dogs in heaven, I'm not going,' though whether or not I'm admitted to that happy abode won't be entirely my decision. What's definitely the case is that I'm much more likely to get there because I love dogs here on earth, since I'm sure they have turned me into a better person. They've made me more caring, more perceptive and more attentive, not only to other animals, but also to my fellow human beings. They've helped me hate cruelty, love kindness and deepen my awareness of the one consciousness which flows through us all.

It's not that I don't get on with people. I have a wonderful family. I love and respect my wife Nicky, my son and my daughters, and I have many friends and acquaintances whose company I enjoy. I appreciate listening to the memories of elderly people; I enjoy being with children. It's not a matter of comparisons; dogs are just different, special. But I was over thirty before I knew anything whatsoever about them. What, then, drove my wife and me to deliver our hearts into canine captivity?

Like so much else which seems innocuous but ends up turning our life around, it all began when the telephone rang one ordinary April morning. As every rabbi knows, a phone call can mean anything from news of an illness, birth or sudden death, to something as banal as the confirmation of yet another meeting. That day it was Sandra, the sister of a colleague. 'I hear you're thinking of getting a dog,' she began, in tones of greater urgency than the subject appeared to warrant. Her information was correct, with particular emphasis on the word 'thinking'. My wife had grown up on an apple farm in Kent, surrounded by a huge family and many animals. When she was a child, if she didn't come home from school at the usual time, her mother simply phoned all her friends who had puppies or kittens and was sure to find that her daughter was there, playing with the baby animals. She'd had dogs, guinea pigs and even a small alligator. The first time I went down from London to meet her family, I was taken aback by sudden calls of 'hello darling' when no one appeared to have entered the room. I looked up and saw a donkey walking past the window and, realising that it was the object of their greetings, understood that I was among people whose values I could share.

But on the question of dogs, I was still far from decided. I wanted to have a dog, but was nervous about what it would entail. I was also a little bit afraid, ever since my brother and I had hidden behind the firmly closed garden gate whenever the neighbour from up the road came down Douglas Park Crescent, where we'd lived on the outskirts of Glasgow, accompanied by what seemed to me then as a child of five the most enormous boxer with huge eyes and thick, dribbling lips.

Nicky and I visited a couple of rescue centres, but returned unconvinced even by the longing looks of the residents. 'They know, don't they?' Sandra's mother, a lifelong dog lover, had said when she heard we'd visited a shelter. 'They can feel you're judging whether to give them a home and it eats their heart out when you pass them by.' I felt instantly mean. There was one dog to which I had taken a liking. When we came back to see him again the staff said happily, 'Freddy, it's your turn at last.' But we didn't adopt him, and I'm ashamed now to think of how he must have returned lonely and hopeless to his bare pen. Attention and affection had eluded him once more; maybe he would never again lie down to doze after his dinner, his stomach full and his heart replete, without this ceaseless anguish of utter and entire aloneness. How many homeless or neglected children feel like that every day: will no one love me, ever?

Sandra explained that her son had found an abandoned dog in the street. She'd spoken to Battersea Dogs and Cats Home, who said they would keep him for seven days. If by the end of the week he wasn't claimed, they'd apparently told her, they would have to put him down. 'I can't do that to this dog,' Sandra pleaded. 'You need to save him.'

'What kind of a dog is it?' I asked.

'He's a mongrel,' she replied. 'Black, medium-sized, well trained and very good natured.'

I called Nicky. 'We don't want a boy dog,' she said. 'And the problem with a black dog is that you can't see it in the dark. But why don't we go along anyway, just to look?'

That, of course, was our great mistake, an error which brought us almost fifteen years of happiness. It was as if the dog knew that he had only this slim, half-minute opportunity to capture our hearts. We had scarcely sat down when he came running in, tail wagging, licked our faces and rendered all objections irrelevant. Ten minutes later I found myself leading him up the steps to our house. I remember asking myself what had happened to my fear of dogs. The truth is that it had vanished in an instant. The next morning saw me out with my new pet buying food, bowls and dog toys, while explaining to the man at the pet shop that, no, it wasn't us who'd chosen the dog, but the dog who had chosen us. He might perhaps have become our dog: that was a matter on which you would have had to consult him. But we had most certainly become his humans. For the next few weeks we lived in dread of a phone call informing us that his previous owner had finally been located. The dog had taken up residence in our hearts, and his home was to be nowhere else but in our house.

We named him Safi, after hearing about a Rabbi Assaf in Jerusalem whose dog reputedly accompanied him everywhere he went, including to the synagogue.

Safi was our first dog. During a decade and a half of happy companionship we must have followed his black tail for no less than ten thousand miles.

'He's too thin,' said our vet, Geoffrey, when we took Safi in for an initial inspection. 'Give him a bowl of cornflakes in the morning.' I can still see Safi, who went to his eternal rest ten years ago, standing by the fridge waiting patiently for me to pour the milk onto his cereal. 'I'll check him out, though I doubt he's been done,' Geoffrey continued, picking up a scanner. To everyone's surprise, it turned out that Safi had indeed been microchipped. Now a legal requirement in the UK, it was then a rare investment. Geoffrey traced Safi's original owner on our behalf; it emerged that the dog had belonged to an elderly man who'd become ill and had to be hospitalised. His housekeeper had put the dog in her car and dumped him in a part of London with which the animal was unfamiliar. His condition suggested that he had been wandering the streets, desperately seeking food, warmth and asylum, for several days before he was found. Our vet told us, his voice deep with anger, that after hearing that the dog had been taken in by a family who wanted to adopt him, the woman had demanded a significant sum of money. 'First you dump the animal; then you try to blackmail us,' he'd replied, furious, before hanging up.

We heard nothing more from Safi's previous owner. Had it not been for that bad experience, we would have taken him to visit the poor gentleman, whose excellent training indicated that he had loved his four-footed friend. Perhaps the dog had been his closest, even his sole companion in old age. Cats and dogs are often a human's most significant other, effectively their next of kin. 'Kin', I discovered when I looked up the term, is related to 'kind'; perhaps our truest kin are those to whom we are bound through ties of loving kindness, whether or not they are literally our relatives or even belong to our own species. We felt pity for this man who might have been left to worry helplessly about the fate of his dog. We could only hope that the housekeeper had told him that he'd found a good and loving home. As for Safi, he would from time to time approach an old man in the street, hopeful and expectant.

I had no idea how to communicate with a dog. One Sabbath morning when we had returned from prayers and everyone was hungry, I found myself prevented from laying the table because Safi was blocking my way. 'Do please sit down,' I said, or something similarly ineffective, in the polite, if slightly insipid tones with which one might address a respected guest.

'Not like that,' observed my mother-in-law, who had been a primary-school teacher all her working life. 'Sit,' she told Safi, delivering the instruction quietly, but with such firm and total conviction that every single person in the room promptly made for a seat, while the dog sunk obediently onto his haunches.

11

One day, several months after he'd become part of our family, Safi barked at the postman. It was only then we realised that until that moment he had never ever barked, never even once emitted so much as a single, stifled growl. His confidence had been so thoroughly destroyed by the trauma of his abandonment that his voice had been completely silenced. For many further months, he never left our sight, not even to go into the garden to do his business. We had to wait for him and watch over him, like a parent over a toddler. If that was what abandonment could do to a dog, I found myself wondering, what would it do to children? In *Pearls of Childhood*, Vera Gissing wrote about her experiences as a child rescued from Nazi Europe on the Kindertransport. 'Here you shall be loved,' were the first words spoken to her by the woman she came to call her English mummy, when she arrived in the country as a young refugee schoolgirl. She had been separated from her parents, whom she was destined never to see again, uprooted from hearth and home and placed on a train to Britain, where she knew not a single living soul. But many equally bewildered and uncomprehending children never heard any such words or affectionate tones ever again in their lives. I hope our dog understood that here, in our house, he was and would be loved.

Safi had one unusual habit which caused us frequent embarrassment. He loved to swing on ropes. Such an item dangled innocently and annoyingly from a thick branch overhanging the brook not far from where we lived. The moment he realised that we had embarked on the path headed in that direction, his pace would quadruple; there was no point even trying to distract him, and once he had begun to accelerate, the task of catching him up was almost impossible. By the time we drew level, he was happily suspended, his teeth entrenched in the thick knotting of the rope, his paws jiggling backwards and forwards as if he were an intoxicated participant in a canine disco inaudible to the human ear, while a mixture of squeals and yowls issued loudly from his lips. It was impossible to call him off. There was nothing for it but to remove my shoes and socks, roll up my trouser legs and wade into the dirty water of the brook, often watched by a curious crowd of jeering teenagers. It wasn't enough to prise apart his jaws; I had, at the same time, to hold him tightly by the collar, or else he would spring back up in a millisecond and resume his mad and merry swinging. Afterwards, he had to be kept on the lead for several hundred yards, or he would make an instant about-turn and race back to his beloved rope to resume his virtuoso performance.

'Who hanged that dog?' an outraged passer-by exclaimed on one exceptionally humiliating occasion, staring at us accusingly and threatening to call both the police and the RSPCA, before lapsing into laughter when he saw how the dog momentarily let go of the rope, only to jump back up one second later and return to his swaying, yowling oblivion. 'Don't let him go near the brook,' we warned our French friends, who kindly offered to treat Safi to an early morning walk.

'Don't you worry; we'll be back in ten minutes,' they promised, as they waved goodbye. An hour and a half later they returned, chastened, drenched and muttering the Yiddish epithet 'meshugge'. 'Your dog', they said, 'is totally crazy.' They had to admit that they had been warned.

Safi had an enviable capacity for making himself comfortable, irrespective of where we were. He had an – almost – infallible gift for making friends. Once, on a bumpy bus journey across the Isle of Mull, he decided that the most comfortable seat would be on the lap of a woman he had never seen before. He simply climbed up and curled onto her overcoat, mercifully to the lady's delight, as well as Safi's. On another occasion, he even managed to beguile the cook in the hotel next to the holiday chalet in which we were staying. Puzzled by his regular disappearance at eight o'clock each morning, I searched among all the other cabins, calling out his name as loudly as I dared, until I eventually observed him exiting the kitchen of the neighbouring inn by the rear door, cheerfully licking his lips.

Safi also often understood, better than I did, how to keep to a reasonably safe path during long country walks. I once took him out on a frozen midnight just before the New Year. Reaching a crossroads, I simply followed the silver, moonlit stripe of path; it was the only feature I could make out in the glimmering darkness. I recall feeling puzzled a moment later to see the dog looking quizzically down at me from above. It was a couple of seconds before the icy cold penetrated my shocked body and I realised that what I had taken to be an intersecting path was in fact a stream. I had stepped off the bridge straight down into three feet of water. 'Idiot!' the dog must have been thinking, though I like to imagine that he did look somewhat concerned as well.

We were nervous when Nicky became pregnant. Would Safi be jealous? We had always imagined that, God willing, it would be children first 'and then, perhaps, a dog'. Safi, who was a cross between various breeds – Staffie, Labrador, maybe also spaniel? – had too large a nose to be put safely out of joint.

'When the baby arrives, make sure it brings the dog a present,' we were advised. Mossy, our newborn, generously handed over a four-bar KitKat, which we now know was probably poison for the dog. Safi was not sufficiently impressed and promptly jumped into my mother's car. She spoiled him thoroughly for two days before bringing him back home, after which he scarcely put a paw wrong. 'Dog' was Mossy's first word. His second was 'Amen'; not a bad beginning, given the household into which he had been born. The dog and the children grew up together, our precious, beloved family, the children eventually outnumbering the hounds by three to one, until death parted Safi from us. 'The only trouble with dogs', I once read, 'is that their lives are too short.'

I have wonderful memories of those days when our children were small and my parents would join us for Friday night dinners, invariably bringing at least one or two special dishes for the feast and gifts for the little ones, and for the dog. Mossy and Safi would rush up the street to greet them, and I would follow, joyfully watching the delight with which the generations encountered one another. Those, too, were the happiest of years.

Mitzpah became our second dog. Our error this time was to stop during a holiday in Wales next to a small, innocuous sign bearing the words 'Border Collie puppies'. 'Shall we just go and take a look?' we asked the children, words which had a disturbingly familiar ring. Safi, by now fourteen and suffering from hip joint problems, was with us in the back of the car. 'Get a new dog before you lose him,' we'd repeatedly been told. But it felt more like treachery than sound advice, like dating a new man while your husband lay dying.

Safi, however, rather liked the puppies. There was also one fully grown collie, perhaps a year old, who kept bouncing up at us with anxious affection. 'What about him?' I asked the farmer.

'He was brought back to us last week,' the man explained. 'His owner was killed in action in Iraq and the family couldn't cope.' The dog's insistent jumping suddenly felt less like playful banter and more like the bewildered desperation of inconsolable loss. Dogs mourn; dogs, too, can die of a broken heart.

We selected a boy puppy. 'If he's sitting looking out for us when we return, then he's the one,' said Nicky, and there he was, staring out from his enclosure. We took him home in a small cardboard box to make him feel safe. He cried and vomited all the way up the motorway until Nicky laid him on her lap; there he fell fast asleep, warm and snug, to awake to a new family and an urban home far from the South Wales hills.

The children chose the name. We gave them a copy of the Torah, the first five books of the Hebrew Bible, and told them to select a name from the chapters read in the week in which our puppy was born. There were plenty of options; luckily it was not some obscure section of Leviticus but the story of the birth and naming of Jacob's twelve sons. But no, none of these appellations was quite the *nom juste* – not Reuben, or Judah, or Gad, or Joseph. The children rejected them all, although our middle child Libbi would have settled for Naphtali. Instead, they chose Mitzpah, the name for the cairn built by Jacob when he parted from his father-in-law Laban, saying 'May God watch between you and me'. The word literally means 'vantage point' or 'lookout' and the dog was indeed to prove a great watcher with his long snout, huge ears and acute, observant eyes.

17

It was only years later that Nicky googled the name and discovered by chance that it also referred to a type of jewellery popular during the First World War. Soldiers bought it for their wives or sweethearts; the brooch was cut in half and each part inscribed with the word *mitzpah*, which was shorthand for 'May God watch over you and me when we are parted from each other.' In the British war cemetery at Bayeux, I saw a gravestone on which this single word comprised the entire epitaph. The dog was waiting in the car; had it been permitted, I would have taken him to visit the grave. Perhaps this soldier had been a man who had loved dogs. If life in the infinite realms beyond our knowledge permitted the occasional glance back into this lower world, he might have appreciated the visit of an eager, handsome hound.

I called Mitzpah 'Mitzi' for short, an abbreviation which was soon to get me into trouble. I was on the phone to the funeral directors, talking to a woman about the arrangements for a burial, when the dog barked so loudly that I couldn't hear a word she was saying. 'Shut up, Mitzi,' I yelled.

'I beg your pardon,' said the lady curtly, obviously offended. It was only then that I discovered that people could also be called Mitzi. Profuse apologies promptly followed, and the incident became a standing joke between us. I eventually found an opportunity to introduce the two Mitzis to each other, and the pair became firm friends.

Our family knew little about the training of puppies, sheep dogs especially. The advice was to keep them busy: 'Border collies are working dogs; either you give them employment or they become self-employed, and you may find you don't like their choice of occupation.' I fancied that, even if he didn't belong to a shepherd or have any sheep, Mitzpah did at least, by virtue of living in a minister's house, have a flock of his own. But that didn't prevent him from chasing round in circles and spending numerous idle minutes barking at imagined ghosts in favoured corners of the house and garden. 'Mitzpah,' I often wanted to ask him. 'What do you see, hear or smell which we humans are incapable of perceiving?'

Safi came to us well trained; Mitzpah had no manners whatsoever. I had no idea where to begin. Nicky promptly enrolled us for puppy classes. The instructor was brilliant, and eccentric. 'There's no such thing as a stupid dog' was one of his favourite, and frequent, sayings, often uttered while looking mercilessly into the eyes of a sheepish human participant. 'They say money makes the world go round,' he explained one summer morning as he took a twenty-pound note out of his pocket. 'I'll show you.' He called over the largest dog in the class and waved the cash in front of its nose. The animal displayed no interest in the banknote whatsoever. When, however, he took out a small piece of cheese, the dog was instantly enthralled. 'See!' he exclaimed, in a tone of vindication which should have been heard in every bank across the city.

Kadya, our younger daughter, proved to be Mitzpah's most effective educator. She taught him how to roll over, put his paws on her shoulder, walk through hoops and even navigate a seesaw which we had specially constructed in the garden. Nevertheless, he had the measure of us rather more quickly than we got the measure of him. Eleven years later, the dog's education remains a work in progress and I admit to making regrettable errors.

Among my own dubious contributions was my attempt to get Mitzpah used to crowds and noise. To this end, I took him with me into town one rush-hour morning. The underground carriage was packed. Mitzpah, who probably occupied more space than a human being, was generously tolerated by the other passengers and enjoyed several pats on the head. I soon found myself squeezed between the carriage doors and a pretty young lady. She suddenly said, very loudly, 'Who just touched my arse?' whereupon the entire carriage fell instantly silent. Luckily, at that very moment the culprit licked her hands; she looked down and burst into laughter while all around us conversations mercifully reverted to their habitual low-decibel hum.

At first, the way Mitzpah would set off on his so-called walks disconcerted Nicky and me; we were used to Safi, who would amble cheerily back and forth a couple of yards ahead of his humans. Mitzpah is different. As soon as I reach down to release him from the lead, he stops, stock still, head lowered, front paws stretched forward, waiting to be off, the canine equivalent of Usain Bolt on the blocks before the hundred metres. Then he's off at top speed, or at least he was when he was young, out into the trees, the fastest dog in the field. A moment later he's vanished entirely. I look around helplessly and eventually spy an inquisitive face peering from behind the trunk of a distant oak. He thinks I can't see him, but his outsized ears give him away. I've always loved those big ears, ever since he was a puppy. I pick up a stick; then he races a long way off to where he estimates it will land and crouches down to watch me with undeviating attention.

It took us a long time to realise that, born to herding and with generations of experience in his genes, he behaves as if there's a flock of sheep between us. He races off for the nearest wall or hedge, behind which he conceals himself, ready to emerge and chivvy them along.

On one occasion when he was a puppy, we thought we'd lost him for ever on the local green. My wife and I did as we'd been instructed and lay down quietly on the grass: 'Don't go after him and he'll soon come back,' we had been told. We felt like idiots, especially when we became aware that the whole affair was being observed with quiet amusement by a tramp who'd pitched his blanket under a nearby bush. But the method eventually worked, and Mitzpah returned, to our enormous relief. He accompanied me once again, but this time safely on the lead, when we brought the traveller gentleman a bowl of hot soup. 'Pity,' I could imagine the dog thinking. 'If they'd let me off that stupid string I would have drunk that stuff the moment the dish touched the ground.'

After Safi, I thought I could never love another dog again. This has not proved to be the case. Safi slept under the bed; Mitzpah sleeps on it. He is just as much loved, and even more indulged. But he's earned his keep; he accompanied me on a hundred-mile sponsored walk round London in six and a half days. And he walked with me again when I made a pilgrimage from my grandfather's former home in Frankfurt, which he only left when the Nazis forced him to flee for his life, all the way north along the Rhine to where it flows into the sea at Hoek van Holland. All the four hundred kilometres we travelled, Mitzpah danced ahead, walked at my side, slept on the clean duvet of a dozen B&Bs and came with me into every café. One night, when we were both extremely hungry and exceptionally cold, we took refuge in a Chinese vegetarian restaurant. Seeing me puzzle over the menu, the proprietor came over to my table and pointed to a simple rice dish: 'That's what most people order for their dogs,' she said. I promptly went and did likewise. At least on that particular journey, I succeeded in loving my canine neighbour as much as my own self, or possibly even more, as the film-maker who accompanied us observed when he saw me lie down on the floor so as not to disturb the dog, who had made himself comfortable on the sofa.

A third dog came to live with us, on a strictly temporary basis only. Vie was a Labrador puppy on her way to Israel to train as a guide dog for blind people. She needed a foster home for a month, prior to her departure for the promised land. We wondered what Mitzpah would make of this new companion. He did his best to ignore the charming-but-mischievous young rascal, while she, emboldened by the affection she received from all comers, barked at him, pawed at him and did her utmost to provoke him to respond. He would have none of it; only once did I catch them playing together at tug-of-war, pulling away amicably at the opposite ends of a short rope. We were given strict instructions on how and when to feed our puppy, and for once even I was careful to obey. After all, you couldn't have a guide dog lead its charge into a café and then go off to help herself at the buffet. Four weeks after her arrival in our home, she departed to begin the next stage on her path to becoming a guide dog. We subsequently heard that she had qualified as a brood bitch, though regarding the precise nature of the specialised training required, we were never fully informed.

But there are more ways in which dogs help us negotiate life than literally leading us through the streets, and more ways in which we need guidance than being physically unable to see. I am mercifully blessed with good eyesight, yet my dogs have been my guides and helpers in innumerable ways.

When people ask me anxiously, as they consider whether to succumb to their children's ever more persistent petitioning, how much time it requires to walk the dog, I tell them that dogs don't take time, they create it: time to set out among the trees at night; time to take a walk with my wife (and the dog); time for a holiday with my children (and the dog); time to be alone, yet never alone because the dog is with me; time to replay the many voices I've heard during the past day, but on the nuance and meaning of which I haven't had the opportunity to reflect; time to do absolutely nothing; time to be silent; time to pray; time interrupted only by the return of the dog to my side, slinking back out of the darkness, to look up eagerly into my face as if to say, 'Well, then, how about doing just one more merry mile?'

1
Joy

He would walk proudly, tail aloft, in the dog equivalent of a thumbs-up to life

Most dogs love life. They love their walks; and they love their creature comforts when they get back home. What's more, their cheerfulness and affection are infectious; they make those around them love their lives more too. 'It's the best part of the day, walking my dog,' confessed a friend, who only a few months earlier hadn't wanted a dog at all but had yielded unwillingly to her daughter's entreaties. It's hard to remain sad for long with a loving dog by one's side.

Both my dogs relished a journey in the car. It didn't matter how often a trip ended in the disappointment of the supermarket car park, they still invariably assumed the best and jumped onto the back seat with the enthusiastic conviction that they were off to the heath, the forest, or maybe, with a bit of luck, a holiday in the hills.

Whenever we went anywhere green, Safi loved to sing – if, that is, one could call his whining and yelping 'music'. He would begin his aria as soon as we turned off the motorway and slowed down, whenever the smell of trees and grass began to drift through the windows. No doubt it was a canine rendition of 'Sing to the Lord a new song', a dog-psalm in joyous anticipation of rushing through the fields and down through the undulating woodlands to the ripple and splash of the streams. He would run proudly, tail aloft, in the dog equivalent of a thumbs-up to life.

Mitzpah had a different way of showing his delight. The moment he was released from the lead he would spin rapidly round in tiny, slowly expanding circles. 'Don't even ask what he's doing,' said a friend, watching Mitzpah's whirling dog-dance, though I often have wondered exactly that. I think it's just sheer animal zest for life: 'You've kept me cooped up for so long; don't think that just because I'm a dog I love my freedom any less than you do.' The circles turn into an elongated spiral as he moves rapidly further away, then sprints off

26

at a tangent to hide behind a bush, waiting for someone to throw a ball or a branch for him to chase.

His exuberance once even won him a competition, almost. We entered him for the dog five hundred metres at a country show. He proved himself by far the fastest creature in the field and would certainly have been awarded first prize, had he not set off in exactly the opposite direction from every other animal in the heat. He didn't mind; he was just happy to be racing at top speed over the grass, exuberant with the joy of being alive.

But dogs are also susceptible to depression; it overcomes them most frequently when a fellow dog or a family member dies, or when a person they love goes away. Their mournful stare when they see the telltale suitcase says it all. But for the great majority of the time, most dogs are eager to seize the moment, or the Frisbee, or the biscuit. They aren't beset by regrets about the past; they don't appear to worry about the future. 'To be or not to be' is not their problem; they don't let too much thinking get them down. They keep their nose to the ground and get on with life.

Dogs give affection freely, increase the love around them and take no part in family quarrels. I've several times observed how a dog can transform a sad or subdued home and bring back life after sorrow. The animal stands there with the tennis ball in his mouth and a beseeching look in his eyes, as if to say: 'You are going to play with me, aren't you?' I get up with an if-I-must-then sigh, but soon reluctance and resistance drain from my heart as I follow the dog into a simple healing world of parks and trees and lampposts.

'Who is happy?' asked the second-century scholar Ben Zoma, answering his own question simply: 'Those who are contented with their portion.' Most dogs are surely happy.

My dogs have been a living embodiment of the age-old Jewish toast, '*Lechayyim* – To Life!' Not, of course, that they actually drink. Mitzpah always ignores the Sabbath wine, arriving exactly in time for the blessing over the bread. Safi, however, did on one occasion sample the bottle. It happened at a friend's house after we had moved from the lounge to the dining room, leaving our half-finished drinks on the floor. The glasses were evidently wide enough for a dog's tongue, because Safi – about whom we'd forgotten as the conversation became heated – rejoined us reeking of alcohol. Mercifully he was still sober enough to walk a straight line home, or as near to straight as any dog ever made.

A dog's 'To Life!' doesn't need artificial stimulants; it's simply an expression of who they are. Just to think about it makes me happy; sometimes I go to sleep with the picture in my mind of the dog running through the woods and Nicky and I following happily after. Then I wake to find that he's crawled up the bed next to me, and is hitting me with his paw, as if to say: 'Stop wasting time sleeping. Get up and take me outside!'

'It's only four in the morning,' I mutter.

Mitzpah hits me again with his paw: 'And so? It's such a wonderful world!'

2
Companionship

Who is left to sit with them, lie down next to them,
look up at them with love?

'Make yourself a teacher and get yourself a friend'
runs an ancient Jewish adage. I can't imagine it
ever entered the mind of its originator that this friend
could be a hound. But, as the contemporary saying goes,
'A dog is a man's best friend' and, for that matter, a
woman's too. I'm not sure that anyone has ever claimed
that their dog is their best teacher, though there's much
I've learnt from my dogs which no other creature has
been able to make me appreciate.

Companionship

For many older people, a dog is their only companion. Perhaps they've outlived their partner and most of their friends; perhaps their children have relocated to the other end of the world; perhaps their increasing lack of mobility has confined them to an ever-smaller radius of interaction. Who is left to sit with them, lie down next to them, look up at them with love, except their faithful dog or cat? That is why it is so important that homes and sheltered housing should not force those who are already so vulnerable, and whose lives are often so restricted and isolated, to part from their one remaining beloved companion just because it walks on four legs.

It is why, too, the work of organisations such as the Cinnamon Trust is so important. It helps elderly or housebound people to keep their pets by finding volunteers to walk them and care for them when their owners are no longer able to do so without assistance. The trust also finds loving homes for those animals who outlive their humans, bringing peace of mind to the men and women who worry about what will happen to their adored pet after they are gone.

It's not only those who are elderly. The lead article in a recent edition of *The Big Issue* was devoted to 'Our vendors and their incredible best friends'.

'For countless homeless men and women across the country their dog is their lifeline,' it began. 'When I got the dog it turned my life around,' acknowledged one grateful human partner. 'Having a dog gives you a great sense of purpose, having someone to care for and love. She saved my life.' In a BBC programme about coping with life on the street, a man spoke about how individual profiteers and gangs of thugs would threaten him by saying that they would cut his dog; to him it felt even worse than the thought of being hurt himself.

It's not just those who are on their own. Many of us who are blessed with family and friends still find something special in the fellowship of a dog. There are always things one feels one cannot say to anyone; things too personal, too silly, too close to the heart. There are parts of ourselves which feel lonely; there are times when we are on our own. The dog understands, we think, as we call the animal over. 'You come along with me,' we say, as we take down the lead and head out for a walk to mull over some complex, shapeless feeling. We want neither to be on our own nor with anyone who might ask any difficult questions: a dog is just perfect.

Furthermore, unless a dog is a 'one master, one mistress' creature, an 'I'm-sticking-with-you-and-only-you' type, he or she can be a best friend to all the family. Who else will sit and listen quietly to the outpourings of both child and adult, aggrieved teenager and upset parent, as a quarrel dies down into the quieter mulling-over phase after the shouting has passed? Who else will sleep on anyone's bed?

Dogs don't differentiate; they are versatile friends, faithful companions in good times and hard times alike.

'They never let you down,' wrote the TV wildlife presenter Chris Packham in *The Times*, insisting that when the time came he wanted his ashes to be mingled with those of his beloved pets. 'Humans will let you down. Animals won't.'

Dogs don't care about us solely for the benefits they can derive from our fellowship either. An astute rabbinic saying differentiates between love which is conditional on some external factor like passionate attraction or mere convenience, and which is therefore likely to end when that factor disappears, and love which is simply love for its own sake. Of course, dogs want their walks and meals, but at heart what they're after is companionship itself. They want to know they're wanted, and what they give in return is unconditional loyalty and affection.

It's precisely that unqualified desire for companionship which makes so many of us love our dogs so much, and they love us in return. 'Come on, Safi,' I would call, and even when he was old and his back legs hurt him he would make the effort to join us in games on the beach. For a few eager minutes his pain seemed to vanish, and whenever, as piggy in the middle, he made a catch, he would run a lap of honour round the children before we could coax him to give us back the ball. His happiness at being part of the fun restored the strength to his legs.

Dogs don't generally make too many demands on us

either; they aren't constantly asking for pocket money, favours, expensive gear, help with their paperwork, or lifts to the bus stop. Every dog owner knows that one loses the occasional round. 'All right then, Safi, if you really must,' I would ruefully say as I yielded once again to his pleading look, only half begrudging him his urgent need for a walk when I really didn't have the time. Dogs can, after all, outstare their so-called owners, breaking down the strongest resolution. But they don't insist they're right in every argument; they don't put you down, they never lie and they never bear a grudge.

By and large dogs are compliant; they're happy to fit in with our plans. They sit with us when we're in, they follow us when we go out; they play games with us when we're happy and when we're sad they lie down next to us in quiet, unspoken sympathy. Most of the time they're game for what we're game for. They'll walk in the park with us, run in the forest, play on the beach, chase the Frisbee, sit on the passenger seat of the lorry, join in the milk round, and – as the remarkable ITV documentary *The Secret Life of Dogs* showed – even dive off cliffs into the ocean or hang-glide over the Californian hills if those are the pastimes about which their owners are passionate. When the children were little and liked to play at damming streams, Safi would hold his breath, put his head under the water and pick up the biggest, smoothest pebbles in his mouth before depositing them on the bank for the construction team to place in the breach. Then, with unfailing gusto, he would shake himself off next to the nearest unsuspecting grown-up.

Dogs, at least older and more experienced dogs, have a profound intuition. It's not just that they know who's afraid of them, and who likes them and wants to play. They're often able to recognise frailty and vulnerability too, and behave accordingly. During his last illness, my father would greet the dog with a warm, 'Hello Safi,' and a big smile. Safi would sit down at his feet and there they would be, the two of them quietly together, each absorbed in the meditations of his old age. Mitzpah was too young for such understanding; his boisterous frisk-iness frightened my father, who had good reason to fear that the eager puppy would accidentally knock him over out of sheer *joie de vivre*. But now, years later, I think that Mitzpah has also reached the age of wisdom. When I'm low, when I suffer from back pain, he lies down near me, looking at me with his steady, affectionate eyes. 'I love you and I'm worried about you,' he seems to be saying, and his presence makes me feel less unsafe.

Dogs don't judge us by how cool we look, how much we earn, how expensive our house or car is, how well connected we are, or the degree to which we are useful in furthering their ambitions, all ways in which, in this utilitarian age, people are apt to evaluate one another. They judge us simply by how well we love them back. They don't shrink from us when we're not feeling well, avoid us when our days go wrong or disown us when we get old. They love us until we die, and sometimes beyond.

When Kurt Moses returned to his native Holland after surviving the horrors of Auschwitz, he went straight to the house of the man with whom they'd left the family Alsatian, Hanni. Had his beloved dog also managed to come through the war alive? As soon as the front door was opened, he saw a shadow cross the man's face. 'After your family left, Hanni refused to eat,' the man explained. 'One day he ran away again. I went to your home and saw him lying with his back pressed against your front door. When I called, he did not move and I realised that he had died. I think he died of a broken heart.'

Looking back many years later, when he wrote his entry for *Faithful Friends*, Kurt observed that he had never recovered from the loss of that faithful dog. Perhaps his sorry fate epitomised the betrayal of faith itself.

3
Cruelty

I don't understand how people can treat them with calculated and continued cruelty

Every few days I receive an appeal with a picture on the cover of a tormented or neglected dog, or some other tortured animal. In its eyes I see – or think I see – the pained bewilderment of a creature which cannot comprehend that another living being could have chosen to be so deliberately and wantonly hurtful. The letters come from the Blue Cross, the RSPCA, the Humane Society, All Dogs Matter, even the local animal shelter.

'Don't take it personally, she's afraid of men,' my friends tell me when their recently adopted dog backs away barking as I enter their home. 'She was badly treated before someone reported her previous owner and the rescue centre took her in. Speak to her gently and she'll slowly make friends with you.'

I don't understand how people can abandon their companion animals to utter neglect or treat them with calculated and continued cruelty. I do admit that even ordinary dog owners like me know, if we're honest, that when we're upset or frustrated we're liable to speak roughly to our hound, or yank in bad temper on his lead should he stop for what we impatiently judge to be too long to sniff at some intriguing tree root on his walk. We do the same with our friends and family, letting out on them the frustrations and irritations which usually derive from another source entirely. Such behaviour isn't right. I remember my teacher Rabbi Lionel Blue of *Thought for the Day* fame, saying, 'Don't take your anger out on your pooch.' No doubt he would have said the same about our spouses or our children. But such behaviour is usually momentary; a minute later we realise how unfair we've been and apologise. After all, it's shameful for a grown human to show bad temper to an innocent animal.

Persistent abuse is of a different order. Yet perhaps the causes are the same. Perhaps the perpetrators project onto their animals the powerlessness they themselves experience at the hands of life itself, the neglect to which they have felt abandoned by those who brought them into this world, or the hurtfulness and injustice which they feel that destiny has meted out to them. Maybe the dog whose callused flanks carry the testament of burns from boiling water has an owner whom others have scalded with the simmering overflow of their own displaced anger. Take it out on the dog, and what can the dog do to answer back, except flinch and slink away? How can a chained or caged dog escape the ravages of a more powerful, more devious and more calculating human?

Probably people mistreat their animals for the same kinds of reasons they beat or abuse their wives or children; it's part of the same syndrome of domestic cruelty. A vet explained to me that social services asked them to look out for signs of violence on animals and, if necessary, report them. 'The owner brings in a dog with broken ribs and bruises. You ask what happened and he comes up with a story of how it fell out of the window. But dogs almost never fall out of windows; you can see at a glance that this isn't the truth.'

Humans aren't the only species frightened by the ghosts of earlier bad experiences. Mary Oliver's moving poem about her new dog, 'Benjamin, Who Came from Who Knows Where', takes a strikingly insightful and compassionate turn:

What shall I do?
When I pick up the broom
he leaves the room.
When I fuss with kindling
he runs for the yard.
Then he's back, and we
hug for a long time.
In his low-to-the-ground chest
I can hear his heart slowing down.
Then I rub his shoulders and
kiss his feet
and fondle his long hound ears.
Benny, I say,
don't worry. I also know the way
the old life haunts the new.

There is something about the lack of guile and the helpless vulnerability of animals which makes human cruelty towards them especially monstrous. I remember being horrified as a teenager by Dostoevsky's description in *Crime and Punishment* of the man who beats his lean and starving horse, a creature on which he depends, and knows he depends, for his livelihood. He whips it repeatedly across the face, driven by the sadistic need to transpose onto the innocent animal the hurt and injustice which he feels life has visited on him, striking the hapless beast over and again across its beautiful eyes.

We have it within our power to inflict on animals,

both domestic and wild, immeasurable cruelty, suffering unto death, persecution to the irrevocable point of total annihilation. Animals have neither voice nor vote. They have no capacity for organised protest and no means with which to argue back, except through the impact they have on the human heart.

There is also the suffering we inflict on other species, not through deliberate, intentional cruelty, but through our heedlessness. Perhaps we should hear in the floods, droughts, storms and heatwaves with which the earth is beginning to argue back, the protest of nature itself against its exploitation through the greed and carelessness of those who consider themselves its masters. Even then, too few pay too little, and too scant, attention. American Indian Chief Seattle's words call out to us with the warning that, 'If all the beasts were gone, men would die from great loneliness of spirit,' as a result of our own thoughtlessness, self-centredness as a species, violence, greed and stupidity.

In her remarkable book *Chernobyl Prayer*, Nobel prize-winning author Svetlana Alexievich describes life, or what remains of it, in 'the zone', the vast area of the Ukraine contaminated as a result of the explosion of the nuclear reactor in Chernobyl in 1986. She simply listens; listens to the old people who have lived there all their lives, who know nowhere else and refused to be evacuated in the wake of the disaster; to the people who hid in the woods when the buses came to take them away; to members of the teams called in as part of the attempt at rescue and decontamination; to the men and women who would not leave their homes or their cat or their dog behind. Time and again her interviewees refer to the animals: wolves, wild boar, elk and deer have taken over abandoned homes and outhouses. These creatures are now the sole living companions the remaining human inhabitants have left. One after another, these resilient people affirm their newly discovered awareness of a fundamental solidarity: fox and deer, wild bird and human; together they constitute life, struggling against the invisible, flesh-and-bone-pervading death by radiation.

Cameraman Sergey Gurin was sent into the zone to film whatever he witnessed. He was showing his work to a group of children when one of them asked why the animals hadn't been evacuated too. Apparently, there had at some point been plans to move them out, but they had hit upon insoluble problems: 'You might be able to herd out all the animals on the land, but what about those inside the earth: the beetles and worms? And the ones up above us in the sky? How do you evacuate a sparrow or a pigeon?' Since this episode, Gurin only wants to film from the perspective of the animals. What does 'man' look like to them? St Francis, he remembers, treated them as equals. He used to preach to the birds, and the birds, perhaps, used to answer him in their own language, which maybe the great saint even understood? But then Gurin recalls that terrible scene in Dostoyevsky, 'A man lashing a horse "on its meek eyes". A madman! Not on its rump, "on its meek eyes".'

Early ecologists took issue with the Hebrew Bible, blaming God's promise of man's absolute dominion over the animals for the alleged Judaeo-Christian contempt for the environment. But this is a fundamental misreading of the intention of the text. Humans are not made to be masters but trustees, faithful guardians and protectors of God's gift of life to all beings. My personal creed comes from the words of the prophet Isaiah: 'You shall not hurt nor destroy in all my holy mountain.' The mountain represents the entire earth, for what space can there be which is not God's holy mountain, in which God's sacred presence does not reside, within the trees and moors, the wild birds and the animals?

In *The New Monasticism: An Interspiritual Manifesto for Contemplative Living*, Adam Bucko and Rory McEntee list nine vows a person dedicated to an ethical and spiritual life should take. They include the promise 'to live in solidarity with all living beings'. I wonder if it is really possible to live in such a way. Maybe we are ineluctably competitive by nature, simply because, like every other organism, we want to survive and not die, and other creatures have to pay the price when we succeed. I don't know how to shop with due awareness of the true cost of what I buy. What has been the price paid by people, animals and the earth itself for the item I choose; how was it grown or produced, packaged, transported and marketed? I don't know what has to die for me to live another year.

Perhaps we can't escape doing inadvertent harm, but we can and must avoid deliberate cruelty.

The Bible tells how God made garments for Adam and Eve in the Garden of Eden after they realised they were naked and became ashamed. Rabbinic legend describes how their coats were embroidered with pictures of every kind of beast and fowl, so lifelike that when the birds and animals saw them, they imagined they were real and, trustingly, drew near, since all creatures still lived peacefully together in those halcyon days. After the deaths of our first ancestors, the clothes fell into the hands of Nimrod, the 'mighty hunter before the Lord'. He used them to lure the unsuspecting creatures into his presence, then laid into them with his club. He was the first to murder trust.

Most dogs, unless already once betrayed, are deeply trusting. Yet humans abandon them, break their hearts, starve them, confine them in tiny cages soon littered with their own excrement, kill them when they are no longer useful, and even in some parts of the world hang them and watch them die slowly, or cook them, or skin them alive and voyeuristically enjoy their pain.

My grandfather, who survived internment in the Nazi concentration camp of Dachau, refused to call Hitler a pig or a dog. 'It's an insult to the animals,' he said.

I do not know how we can atone for our guile, our

sadism or our wilful neglect, or how we can ever make good the effects of our violence against the fellow beings who would gladly have walked by our side, grazed in the fields, or sung from the uprooted trees.

Haunted by his wanton killing of just one bird, Coleridge's Ancient Mariner comes to a simple conclusion:

> *He prayeth best who loveth best*
> *All things both great and small.*

Adjusting to a new home

He'd never been near a Christmas tree before.
The silence . . . was excruciating

To describe how we found our dogs would be to address only one side of the question; no less important is how the dogs found us. In particular, what did life look like for a dog discovered on the street, or uprooted from his native Welsh hills, and deposited without prior consultation in a rabbinical household?

I am a rabbi, a minister of religion in the Jewish community, privileged with the responsibility of serving my congregation, my people and whoever I may be able to help. Judaism, like all true faiths, teaches us to love God through loving and caring for God's creation. I visit the sick, endeavour to support the bereaved, and study and teach our sacred texts. I strive to understand from my religion how to do what is good, kind and just. I try to learn from people of all creeds and none, and from the world around me, including the animals too.

As in all faiths, Jewish life turns around prayer, study and care for others. Its rhythm is fixed by the weekly Sabbath and the annual cycle of festivals. But at all seasons, home, family and community are central, and the most frequent gathering place is the table, laden with seasonal dishes. There can be no doubt that from a dog's point of view, food forms the core of the religious experience, though prayer and the synagogue are not entirely irrelevant.

When I told my own teacher that we'd taken on a dog, or rather that a dog had taken over us, he told me the following story. An orthodox rabbi was serving a strictly pious congregation, whose members all frequently asked him questions about whether particular foods were, or were not, kosher. All, that is, except for one man. The rabbi was curious to know the reason for his reluctance. 'Well,' the man explained, 'it says in the Bible that you should give non-kosher food to your dog to eat. Whenever I'm unsure if something is or isn't kosher, I test it by putting some of it down in front of the dog, who I'm sure understands that he's only supposed to eat it if it is non-kosher. If he refuses to touch the stuff,

I take that as proof positive that it must indeed be kosher.' A year passed by and the gentleman began to ask questions of the rabbi, just like everyone else.

'*Nebbich*,' said the rabbi, a Yiddish expression for 'poor thing', 'has the dog died?'

'No,' the man replied, 'it's just that he's become extremely strict.'

I suspect that dogs in Jewish households do rather well, probably unhealthily so, when it comes to food. Mitzpah's favourite moment comes with the blessing of the Sabbath loaves, the challah, on Friday night. He even seems to have acquired the relevant Hebrew, because he never appears at the wrong liturgical moment. But as soon as we begin to perform the ritual washing of the hands preceding the breaking of the bread, a large nose emerges above the side of the table, slowly edging upwards, followed by an eager mouth and unwaveringly focused eyes. I've trained him to offer a paw when you say 'Shabbat Shalom', a canine variant of singing for your supper, prior to rewarding him with his first piece of the soft, delicious bread. Following this *hors d'oeuvre* he makes an underneath-the-table tour of the collected company before selecting, with invariable success, the two or three most gullible members.

Like all dogs, Mitzpah is constantly on the lookout for ways of supplementing his daily rations, sometimes with choice items and sometimes with items which shouldn't be of any dog's choosing. He's learnt that his moment of opportunity arrives when I'm saying goodbye to visitors and the dining room is left unattended. Chairs are generally abandoned at precisely the correct distance from the table to provide an intermediate platform for climbing up and helping himself. In this manner, he has with selfless consideration spared his humans many unhealthy calories.

Less appealing was his penchant in younger days for socks, tights and *kippot*, the skullcaps worn by traditional Jews as a sign of respect before the presence of God. The latter would duly reappear in the middle of unpleasant heaps in the garden, leaving the question of whether, after a couple of turns in the wash, it was fitting to wear them once again. Tights were more of a problem; there are things on which it's evidently hard for even a canine sphincter to get a proper grip. That was how Nicky found herself outside the synagogue one bright Sabbath morning, accompanied by a dog from whose backside the telltale fabric of such a garment was reluctantly emerging. She had no other recourse but to ask one of the children to hold the dog's collar, while, hand over hand, she gingerly withdrew the offending item from the thoroughly offensive creature. By the end of the operation she found herself standing at a distance of over two metres from the animal's backside. Mitzpah was no doubt gazing back over his shoulder with a look of innocent bewilderment, as if to say: 'Wherever could that have possibly come from?'

Safi was known across the community for his unfailingly friendly welcome. He embodied the value of hospitality to guests – so long as they were human. He had a somewhat different attitude to other dogs that were unwise enough to intrude on his patch. Even when his hips were failing, he would invariably clamber carefully down the stairs to greet every new person who arrived in the busy house. Only when he became too ill to negotiate the steps would he wait at the top for me to carry him down. He was universally loved by the congregation, who honoured his passing by naming after him the Israeli guide dog for whose training they were raising funds.

Both dogs acquired a basic familiarity with the seasons of the Jewish year. But in this art, it was Mitzpah who excelled. He knows when it's Passover, the festival before which, in accordance with the biblical injunction to eat no leavened foods, we rigorously remove all bread, biscuits, cereals, pasta and flour-based products from the house. He especially enjoys the ritual of 'searching for the leaven', the ancient custom of checking that the house is truly free of all proscribed products. The practice is to search the home by the light of a candle at dusk on the night before Passover for any remaining undiscovered crusts and crumbs. To ensure that the activity is taken seriously, a small piece of bread is concealed in each room prior to the search. In our family, the women generally do the hiding and the men the looking; Mitzpah, who counts among the latter, offers his team a considerable advantage since he frequently sniffs out the hidden pieces well before his humans find them. One year, he even took the initiative and began the process all on his own, with the result that when it came to the hour for searching, not a single piece of the hidden bread remained anywhere to be seen.

As for matzah, the unleavened flatbread eaten during Passover, he's none too fond of that. 'Not that stuff again,' he seems to say with his disappointed look when we pass him his first piece of the dull, brittle substance. But he doesn't dislike it sufficiently to refuse to eat it altogether. This is just as well, as Passover is something of a canine occasion, since the Bible notes that on the night when the Children of Israel left Egypt not a single dog barked. It's no doubt a sign that even dogs believe in freedom and deplore slavery. Indeed, in 1979 the Farm Animal Welfare Council of the UK formulated a charter of freedoms for animals living under human control, including freedom from hunger, thirst, injury, disease, pain, discomfort, fear and distress, and 'the liberty to express normal behaviour'. These are freedoms which innumerable human beings throughout the globe would desperately love to possess.

The Jewish New Year, which falls in September or early October, brings problems of its own. Mitzpah is definitely not fond of the shofar, the ram's horn blown as a memorial before God, the central rite of the festival.

The note it produces is something between a rasp, a whine and a prolonged and piercing cry. To humans it is strangely and deeply affecting, as if nature itself were crying out in anguish before God. As the twelfth-century philosopher Maimonides wrote, it's a wake-up call to the soul to be mindful, just and compassionate. It most certainly arouses the dog. When he hears it, Mitzpah at first growls quietly, then progresses to barking back at the injurious sound, the harsh cry and high pitch of which is no doubt offensive to his large and sensitive ears, before finally resorting to competition, prolonging his whining retaliation for several seconds after the horn has fallen silent.

The New Year is followed just one week later by the Day of Atonement, a strict fast from dusk until nightfall on the following day. Dogs, like all other animals, are not commanded to participate. In fact, one of my favourite sounds on the twenty-five-hour fast without either food or liquids, is of the dog lapping up his water. It quenches some inner anxiety in me, some visceral dread which I experience most acutely in times of drought, when the grass turns yellow and dead leaves cover the pavement well before the cold of autumn; a fear that the very earth will cease to be benign and generous, in retaliation for our contempt for its needs and beauties and for the non-human life it sustains.

The fact that they are not obliged to fast does not imply that dogs have nothing of which they need to repent on this day of remorse and reconciliation. Dogs definitely possess a conscience; anyone who's seen a guilty hound creep stealthily under the table knows all too well that dogs know right from wrong. It could be argued that these moral categories derive not from any inner ethical sense, but rather from what their owners have inculcated in them since puppyhood. But then the question of whether morality is intuitive or culturally conditioned is not limited to the consideration of canine conduct alone.

Safi was definitely a dog more sinned against than sinning. One misdemeanour of which he was undoubtedly guilty, however, took place when Hungarian friends telephoned unexpectedly to tell us that they happened to be in town that afternoon. We offered to collect them and go for a winter walk, accompanied by the dog. Afterwards we left Safi in the car while we went for a welcome coffee. As we were dropping our friends back where they were staying, they kindly informed us that they had brought us a special gift of two large cakes, baked according to an ancient Hungarian Jewish recipe. They had left them in the back of the car. It was at this moment that I noticed the trail of crumbs across the floor of the vehicle and a large, empty white bag. I was fool enough to add insult to injury by bursting out in laughter. At first our friends were offended, but they soon regained their normal generosity of spirit when we realised that the story of the incident of the dog and the pastries was likely to have a much longer shelf life than the cakes would have had on their own. As for Safi, he lay on his back for three days, his stomach hot to the touch, before throwing up in my study on the holy Sabbath. I couldn't bring myself to blame him, though; it wasn't entirely his fault if he was led so thoughtlessly into temptation.

The autumn harvest festival of Tabernacles is probably Mitzpah's favourite celebration, when we eat our meals outside in the succah, an improvised harvester's hut constructed specially for the eight-day feast, decorated with the flowers and fruits of the year and covered with a roof made of branches and leaves. The colder the weather, the more the guests appreciate the dog's presence, since he provides welcome foot-warming services by lying down on their shoes. In return he can usually expect the reward of the odd accidentally dropped pieces of challah and other delicacies.

But it would be wrong to give the impression that it was only the food that mattered to them; the dogs related eagerly to many other aspects of their rabbinical lifestyle as well.

Both dogs loved to accompany me to prayers. I had only to call out 'synagogue', or '*shacharit*', the name of the morning service, and Mitzpah would invariably come running. I only wish the appeal would be equally effective with the two-legged members of the community. He sleeps happily in my study until the prayers are over, an opportunity no doubt envied by some of the human participants in the dawn congregation. If I know that everyone in attendance is comfortable with dogs, I occasionally let him doze in the corner of the room where we pray. He lies there, eyes closed, for all the world profoundly immersed in the liturgy of praises to God who made heaven and earth, the wild and domestic animals, the birds of the air and the fishes in the sea. His presence, when he doesn't misbehave, is deeply calming. A friend who had recently lost her sister spent an entire service sitting quietly next to him. 'That dog', she said afterwards, 'was exactly what I needed.'

A canine talent of which I failed to take due advantage is connected to the requirement in Jewish prayer of a minyan, a quorum of ten adults. Traditionally this would have consisted of ten men; nowadays many communities, including mine, count women equally. But what was to be done if, at the crucial moment in the service when the ten were needed to enable the recital of the most sacred prayers, one person or more was lacking? If I'd thought of it when he was young, I would have trained Mitzpah to leave the synagogue with a note attached to his collar saying 'two more urgently needed', and bark outside the front doors of the houses of congregants living on the same block, alerting them to the indispensable importance of their immediate attendance.

A key privilege in the Sabbath service, and also on certain weekdays, is to be called to the reading of a portion of the Torah. The person chosen for this role is required to recite short blessings before and after the reading. I once jokingly asked the man responsible for the allocation of this honour if he would call up my dog. 'Of course,' he replied. 'Just let me know when you've taught him the blessings and I'll put him on the list.'

The dogs also took full part in study activities in our home. Safi, in particular, showed a persistent interest in Jewish learning. He faithfully attended virtually all my classes, carefully positioning himself to best advantage. Every Thursday morning, he would sit behind my friend David, sadly since gone to his eternal rest, not just because he was a true scholar, but mainly because he expressed his adoration of God's creatures by surreptitiously slipping the dog an unconscionable quantity of biscuits. 'It's not good for his waistline,' we'd say, but our words fell on deaf ears . . . and on a large, open mouth.

On Wednesday evenings, when the room was often packed with students, Safi preferred to lie underneath the table, where he could absorb his lessons in undisturbed meditation. One day, an unfortunate and especially pungent smell emerged from down below and drifted unpleasantly across the room. 'Safi! Out!' I said firmly, lifting the edge of the tablecloth to check on his precise location. But the dog was not in the room.

Dogs who accompany their minister-humans require certain interfaith skills. Of these, Safi did not always prove himself capable. While sleeping for the duration of a service of any denomination is well within the capacity of most dogs (and many humans), knowing how to react to previously unfamiliar religious symbols requires a degree of discrimination and forbearance. In Safi's defence, he'd never been near a Christmas tree before. His instinctive conclusion, that 'if there's a tree it means I'm outdoors', was only too understandable. By the time I had shouted at him to stop, the telltale evidence of his misdemeanour was dripping from the ribbons and wrapping paper of an entire pile of presents. The silence while I carefully wiped them down with an undersized tissue was excruciating.

But, more than anything else, the dogs created a special place for themselves as welcomers and greeters. Occasionally their skills fell short, and I would take them upstairs and firmly shut the door to protect them from what they experienced as the invasion of too many humans. But, on the whole, they were helpful. Many people are inevitably nervous when they go to see the rabbi. I don't think of myself as intimidating, but my rabbinic title is; I often hear the comment: 'It isn't you, it's the role.' Walking into a hallway with a dog wagging his tail or rolling over to have his tummy tickled makes a rabbi's or a vicar's home more welcoming and the entire experience more relaxed. Without saying a single syllable themselves, they turn the minister into the kind of creature with whom you might feel you could actually talk, and who would listen with sympathy if you chose to pour out your heart.

But without doubt the greatest contribution the dogs have made to the rabbinic profession is through what they have given to me. When I feel low, I call the dog; he sits down next to me and seems to understand. I'm sure he doesn't fathom the issues: how to manage the next meeting, why the previous encounter went badly, or what I need to say to repair a fragile relationship. But it's not for his advice that I need him; it's because he makes me feel less alone, gives me the confidence that, somehow, I can cope. Safi used to lick my face; Mitzpah lies down near me and rolls over to have his stomach stroked. If I stop, burdened with other preoccupations, he hits my hand with his paw until I resume. But whatever their method, both dogs have understood how, in ways far simpler and more palpable than God's more recondite and frequently imperceptible methods, to restore my soul. Or perhaps dogs are part of God's armoury, God's agents and servants, just as we are, albeit in different ways.

4
Prayer

I sometimes sit down next to the dog and spread my black and white prayer shawl over his head and mine

O ne could be forgiven for thinking of it as a burden, part of the bad luck of ending up in a rabbi's house, but both Safi and Mitzpah loved to come with me to prayers. After all, why should a pleasant early morning walk be spoiled by a lazy three-quarters of an hour spent waiting while one's human goes through the strange ritual of addressing the infinite in an abstruse language, under the illusion that there might actually be someone out there listening. For both Safi and

Mitzpah, a walk was still a walk and the early morning scents were cool and fresh. (It was Mitzpah who was with me in the shop on the shores of Loch Ness when I muttered something about Loch Ness Monster T-shirts, pencils, mugs, soft toys, notebooks, and all this money being made from a creature whom no one could prove actually existed. I had obviously mouthed my words louder than I thought, because someone turned and asked me, 'And what do you do for a living?')

More importantly, though, both dogs helped me not simply to get to my prayers, but also to focus more deeply on them once I was there. That's because of the special gift dogs have for concentration.

Dogs aren't good at multitasking. It may sound like a defect, but it's one of the things I respect about them. The ability to do several things at once seems to me an overrated virtue. Of course, there are times when one doesn't have a choice, like the parent who has to keep one eye on a crying three-year-old, the other on a restless five-year-old threatening to run out into the street in front of a car, and the eyes in the back of his head on the warden examining whether or not he's parked on a yellow line. Sometimes, too, multitasking can be liberating; after all, many of the best conversations take place in the kitchen, where keeping the hands busy peeling potatoes somehow creates the right atmosphere for a heartfelt conversation. But all too often multitasking means doing neither activity with proper concentration. It's the sign of a distracted consciousness, a symptom of the over-stimulated, under-focused bewilderment of our times. The result is a wearying form of ceaseless low-grade dysfunction.

There's a special art to doing just one thing, at one time, with the whole of one's self. To appreciate what that looks like, all one has to do is watch a dog staring at a biscuit. Every facet of its being, the alignment of its head, the gaze of its eyes, the poise of its posture, are all directed at that small but infinitely desirable object. Hebrew has a word for such concentration, *kavvanah*. It literally means direction, or focus. To do something with *kavvanah* means to give the deed one's full attention. It's particularly important in the context of prayer. 'Prayer without *kavvanah*,' wrote Abraham Joshua Heschel, the modern-day mystic and civil-rights activist who marched in Selma, Alabama, next to his close friend Reverend Dr Martin Luther King, 'is like a body without a soul.' Anybody who practises the discipline regularly understands that to pray with true concentration, with one's whole heart and undistracted consciousness, is not a simple matter. It can't be achieved by deliberate effort alone, because then one ends up thinking about thinking, but it cannot be attained without disciplined endeavour either.

Maybe that's why on days when I feel that I'm far from succeeding, I sometimes sit down next to the dog and spread my black and white prayer shawl over his head and mine. Then he, intuitively understanding that this is something sacred, something to which silence and stillness pertain, lies next to me without stirring. The two of us form a small but warm-hearted unit, a fractal of the great at-oneness that animates and embraces all living things.

And, just occasionally, when I'm ill and can't attend the synagogue for communal prayers, I create a mini-communion consisting of my dog and me, and I curl up next to him, or he curls next to me, and we say our prayers together. For what is prayer but this: thankfulness for the gift of living, for the ability to feel and think, see and hear, touch and smell on this miraculous earth, for the gift of one's heartbeat within this limitless pulse of existence, which fills all beings with life, withdraws its tide at death, and brings renewal to shores we will never know. But meanwhile we have run, and sung, and barked, and played, and been thankful. What is prayer but this connection, and this gratitude?

At other times I pray while Mitzpah and I walk or run together. I have to admit that it's certainly not what the legalists had in mind when they determined the proper degree of devotion in which the liturgy was supposed to be recited. I match the rhythm of the ancient words to my pace and, in my better moments, concentrate carefully on each individual phrase. There's a wakefulness to the world at night; the day has withdrawn its distractions and the woods and fields breathe out in relief, in silent, vibrant meditation. This secret vitality calls out in the stillness, or in the wind, or with the movement of the branches and leaves. My spirit answers in companionable joy, in shared prayer deeper than the words of any specific praise or petition; in that simple, purifying communion which the author and healer Rachel Remen describes as 'a connection on the deepest level with the largest possible reality'. Mitzpah is part of that reality, and, as he runs back to my side from the edge of the next field, he seems to feel it too.

I don't know if the dog also prays, or what a canine liturgy might look like, except that it would surely contain the wish that people would treat them kindly and with respect, go for more and longer walks, and leave food unguarded with more frequent carelessness. Or perhaps, in the long hours when they're left alone, they pray naturally and unselfconsciously for love, and that their two-legged friends, so often faithless, should not forget them. They would no doubt include at the core of their meditations the desire that their humans, under whose control they have fallen, should at least aspire to love their dogs as themselves, if not more. How am I to know if, without even being conscious that he is doing so, my dog doesn't pray more deeply and naturally, more totally with all his being, than me?

I feel safer on these night runs when the dog is at my side. Where he won't go, I don't go either. It's not just God who makes me feel secure. The dog leads me through dark and winding paths, green pastures, singing streams and tranquil waters too. I don't know about goodness and mercy following me, but it's blessing enough to be pursued by eager ears and a happily wagging tail.

The medieval thinkers described different levels of soul, ranking the 'animal' far below the 'speaking' or the 'intellectual'. No doubt that's true in the refined dimensions of philosophy. But on the wavelength of the heart, through love and *joie de vivre*, the dog frequently awakens in me a vivid sense of the commonality of life itself, embracing animals and humans, birds and trees. When I think of God, it's that ceaseless flow of being which I mean; the inexhaustible well of existence manifest in people, dogs, rivers, fields and seas.

With his joy and affection, his trust and need for love and attention, the dog evokes in me a deep sense of companionship, transcending the solely human. It's a fellowship shared by the horses in their dark fields too, their warm breath rising like thin mist. It draws me closer to whatever the source may be of both Mitzpah's life and mine, and of everything that exists. Sometimes it's the contact with an animal through which we come to feel a special kinship, or maybe it's even a favourite tree, which makes us aware of what is around us and within us the whole time. Yet without that relationship, without that bond with another form of life, we would be unable to experience this mysterious unity. Maybe that's what Eleanor O'Hanlon meant when, in her beautiful book, *Eyes of the Wild: Journeys of Transformation with the Animal Powers*, she describes her encounter with grey whales as an opening through which there pours 'a wordless sense of connection with a greater life.'

5
Love

Like humans, dogs need not only to be loved, but also to be shown that they are

'I love you,' I hear myself say to the dog, often with a frequency with which I feel embarrassed, so that I catch myself looking behind me to check that no one else has heard. Sometimes I even answer myself, pretending to be the dog, telling myself in would-be canine tones, 'I love you, too.' If this is a sign of madness, then there are a lot of insane people, since I've noticed many other dog fans doing the same, or at least the first, less-crazy, part. I recently overheard my wife replying to one of the children who justly moaned that I was overdoing it: 'At least at four every morning you don't have to hear, "I love you so much", and I think he's talking to me; but no, he's speaking to the dog who's just jumped on the bed and woken me up.'

'I love her so much; the weeks without her have felt endless,' a man confesses in the waiting room at the vet's, apologising for being so sentimental. 'I'm longing to see him again. I don't know what I'll do with myself if he doesn't get better,' a lady tells the veterinary nurse at reception, taking out a handkerchief to wipe away her tears.

It's always important to tell those for whom we care just how much they mean to us. Never taking our loved ones for granted is advice few of us take sufficiently to heart. 'I loved her so much. I only wish I'd told her more often, but now it's too late' are devastating words to hear at a funeral.

But, somehow, it feels easier to tell our love to the dog, unfair to our human family as that is. Why do so many people love their dogs so simply and so much? What art is it, which so many dogs possess, what skill or subterfuge, which enables them to crawl so quickly and deeply into one's heart? By the time one realises what's happened, one isn't able, and doesn't want, to get that dog back out again.

'It's those big brown eyes,' says Nicky, watching the dog take advantage of my better judgement once again.

It's with that unblinking, directly-at-you, straight-to-the-soul stare that dogs tell you, not so much that they love you, but, more importantly, that you simply have to love them, that you haven't got a choice, that it would be unthinkable, unimaginable, beyond all possible justification if you failed to fall for their charms. I admit that I'm gullible. But, then, there are many worse characteristics to possess. If it came to a choice, I'd rather be credulous than cruel.

Perhaps it's the dependency and trust, the lack of guile of domesticated animals in contrast to the calculated manipulations of humankind. Aharon Appelfeld, the Holocaust survivor and novelist, wrote of how through all the nights of terror when he hid in barns and hayricks to evade the SS, and their many local allies who in those lean and terrifying years would gladly have earned their meagre reward from the Nazis for handing over a Jew, the only time he ever felt safe was among the cows and sheep, the horses, cats and dogs, close to whom he secretly crept, then slept the deep and easy sleep of a child, confident that these creatures would never betray him. They knew no duplicity or deceit.

It's not that the connection with a favourite animal is deeper than the bond between people. But it's a different, easier kind of love. It may lack much of the subtlety, tenacity, self-sacrifice, sensitivity, exaltation, bliss, and extent in years and range of shared activity that a faithful and sustained relationship with a fellow human being may attain. But it doesn't have the tension and ambiguous complexity of human relationships either. When a pet dies, we miss our four-footed friend profoundly. But we are not usually spliced apart and left with one whole side of our ribcage torn and bleeding and our heart exposed to the wind and cold, as we are when we lose our life's closest human companions. Unless, as sometimes happens, we find it easier to weep for such a clear, uncomplicated loss as the death of our beloved dog, and our tears flow unchecked and uncheckable, as they refused to do when our human relative died.

Maybe it's that sheer simplicity, that absence of ambivalence and conflict, in how one loves a dog. There's little clash of self and other, of what he wants against what she wants, of altruism and egotism. The bond with a dog is unweighted by the burden of excessive expectations, free of all the endless words and silences and the inferences and misunderstandings to which they give rise. We don't have to see in our dog, as we do, if we are honest with ourselves, in our children, the effect not just of our love and strengths of character, but also of our failures and vulnerabilities. If we wake in the middle of the night contrite and tearful over our failings, or our frustrations at those of others, the dog, if he's nearby, will simply lick away our tears, or crawl closer to have his tummy tickled. He'll make no call on our capacity for remorse and shame.

Maybe it's the fact that dogs don't respond with their own ego, don't compete with us by interrupting our flow with a story of their own: 'Oh, the same thing happened once to me, only in my case it was incomparably worse.'

Maybe it's the steadfastness of the companionship. 'Where you go, I go,' says Ruth to her mother-in-law Naomi in the book of the Bible which bears her name. Even when Naomi repeatedly entreats her to return to her homeland and the family of her birth, she refuses to be parted from her side. 'No,' says Ruth. 'Where you lie, I lie.' Dogs are faithful followers in her footsteps.

It's the day-by-day here-I-am constancy of the affection of a dog. With what other living being does a person spend so much time, share so many hours, as with the dog who's always by one's side? It's the unwavering loyalty. It's the absolute trust. It's the reliable affection. It's the tail-waving, body-wagging, eyes-staring-up-at-you total and joyful greeting when you come home. It's the readiness to get up and follow, wherever you are going.

It's the unconditional love – unconditional, that is, so long as you feed them, walk with them, and love them in return.

It's precisely because that love is so absolute and trusting that it's such a profound sin to betray it. A dog puts its life in the hands of its owner. To treat it with deliberate cruelty is therefore an act not only of brutality, but of betrayal. It's a cruel sin to bring a child into the world and then to refuse it love and nurture. It's also wrong to take a dog into one's home, and then beat it, scream at it, and throw it out, helpless, onto the street.

Safi went through a prolonged phase during which he would sit down next to one of us and insist that we held his paw. 'It's a new thing with him,' my mother observed. 'He looks at you, lifts up his paw and waits until you take it.' No doubt he needed this gesture of solidarity to heal the inner anguish left over from his abandonment when scarcely more than a puppy. That it lay within our capacity to resist occurred, of course, to neither my mother nor to me; to spurn his outstretched paw felt like a display of heartlessness. This is not to say that it wasn't often a nuisance. Safi's solicitations were especially inconvenient when he chose to sit himself down on the floor close to your pillow, his leg held up towards you like the hand of a frightened child, leaving you wondering how to support your bedtime book and turn the pages with one arm permanently immobilised in a prolonged gesture of canine reassurance.

Mitzpah had a different way of demanding affection. If you stopped tickling his tummy he would simply prod you repeatedly with his paw until you recommenced. Nicky was once so absorbed in her reading that she failed to comply with his wishes when he rolled over at her feet. He stood up, cross but in no way nonplussed, and, employing his long snout, whacked her book shut, before rolling over again in a second, more successful, attempt at blackmail.

Like humans, dogs need not only to be loved, but also to be *shown* that they are. 'The first thing I do in the morning when I get out of bed is go over and kiss my dog,' a friend recently confessed to me. 'It brings me great comfort. People who don't have dogs just don't get it, do they?' I can well imagine that they truly don't. Dogs give grown men and women permission to be sentimental, to admit, unashamedly, though preferably without being overheard, how much we crave love. Maybe that's an opportunity, an outlet, which all of us need – though which of us would want to admit it in public?

Or maybe it's the way a dog can open the heart, the simplicity of feeling which a dog's unequivocal trust and devoted companionship engenders, which brings us the gift, not just of being loved, but of feeling that we, too, are capable of being loving.

It's sad when someone goes to his grave with his capacity for love unfulfilled. Imagining there really is a God who gives us a post-mortem interview, one of the questions would probably be: 'How much did you love?' It would be tragic if we had to reply, 'Not a lot really. I only used about twenty per cent of my heart.' Dogs certainly help us raise our grades.

Most of our love is rightly directed towards our fellow humans, our family first, our friends, neighbours and the strangers in our midst. But maybe every human heart also contains a specific place, just a corner, which is only fulfilled through the love of God's creatures: animals, birds, trees and flowers – but most especially dogs.

6
Rules

'Soon,' I say.
'It won't be long now.'

'Habits', a friend said to me once, 'are good things to have on your side.' She certainly wasn't thinking about dogs, but rather about Judaism, with its rules and traditions about how to approach even the smallest details in life. For, as another friend used to say, 'life is made up of little things', and there's nothing so insignificant that it can't be done either with ill-will or with good grace.

Dogs, too, like their rules and routines. When Vie,

the future guide dog, came to stay with us at eight weeks old, we were given strict instructions on what to do. She was to sleep in her crate, eat at specific times after we called her with a clicker, and be taken out to the garden to do her business with the instruction 'bizzy, bizzy'. At first I thought the crate was cruel; I quickly found that Vie loved it, together with all the signs, signals and keywords that structured her life. She knew where she was, she felt safe; and dogs and humans both feel better when they know where they stand.

Although often indulged (I am the main culprit), our dogs have been reasonably obedient. Safi came to us beautifully trained. He would step cautiously off the pavement to do his poo, wait patiently while we sorted his food and generally come as soon as we called him. He did show an increasing capacity for selective hearing as he grew older, a gift he had in common with a large number of humans of every stage of life. But in emergencies he listened. Once, on the way home from Scotland, we stopped overnight at a farm. Without realising it, I had parked right next to the hen house, so that when I opened the rear door Safi jumped straight in among the chickens. There was an instant cacophony; feathers flew in all directions. Mercifully, though, Safi retreated immediately at the sound of our yells, and no lasting damage was done.

Mitzpah was, at first, rather unruly, but he gradually became more biddable, with exceptions. He knows he's not allowed to lie on the newly reupholstered furniture in the lounge, but that the old red sofa in the kitchen is his for the taking. He waits when I tell him to, if I express myself firmly enough, and comes to heel when I call, though he has a strange idea of quite how far in front of me my feet extend. Sadly, he has never quite grasped the instruction that barking is strictly forbidden before eight o'clock in the morning.

But by and large he recognises and appreciates his routines and the rhythms of the different days of the week. On the Sabbath, for example, he knows that I get up first and sit downstairs at the hall table to prepare for the synagogue services. He knows that this is the morning when I take him out to the nearby green for an early walk. He watches my every move, sighing pointedly whenever I reach for yet another book. 'Soon,' I say. 'It won't be long now,' as he looks at me in quizzical disbelief. I do my best never to let him down.

I was a teacher before I became a rabbi. Though secondary trained, I ended up working with infants. I quickly learnt that children both need, and like, to know where the boundaries lie. I read somewhere that if all explanations fail, one should say, as firmly as one can: 'Because!' To my amazement, it worked. Children feel relieved when there's someone in charge, so long as he or she is reasonably fair. Dogs are the same.

But there's a deeper importance to rules than demarcating routine. I became sharply aware of this on my first visit to Germany. The child of refugees from Nazism, I was asked if I hated being in the country in which my family had been persecuted fifty years earlier. In fact, my feelings were rather different: I returned home not with anger but with an acute respect for law. Horrified by what ordinary people had done under the Nazis, I found myself reflecting on the privilege of living in a country in which the laws are, by and large, fair. Just laws prevent us from engaging in acts of which, were we to be permitted or incited to commit them, we might regrettably prove capable. Only a fool assumes himself immune to the influence of prejudice and hatred. Law protects us not only from the wrongs others may inflict on us, but also from the evil which we ourselves might commit.

Dogs, too, need to be prevented from doing the worst that lies within their nature. I learnt this the bad way with Mitzpah. A friend told me that I ought to practise, while he was still a puppy, taking Mitzpah's food bowl away from him while he was in the middle of eating. I didn't get it; I simply failed to understand why this might be an important exercise. The result is that I have to keep a watchful eye if there are guests around while Mitzpah's having his meals, because I can't be sure that he won't take unkindly to anyone appearing to come between his mouth and his food. It may be only natural to defend one's dinner plate, but 'only natural' is not a good enough reason. It may, after all, be only natural for human beings to fight, steal and kill; it is to something rather higher than our blind, instinctive nature that we aspire.

Mitzpah was still a puppy when we first took him to Scotland. One day he hurt his paw and we took him to the local veterinary surgery. 'Border collies', the vet observed, 'often suffer from nervous aggression.' The comment made every sense to us; we'd witnessed how he'd sometimes show his teeth when he was anxious. Now that we understood, we were able to manage his anxiety better, and keep him happier, calmer and safer. Perhaps the reason human beings are sometimes pugilistic is that we, too, suffer from nervous aggression. We don't really mean to be sharp and nasty; it's just that we feel uncomfortable and uncertain and respond by snapping at whoever is unfortunate enough to be next to us at the time. But it's not a good enough excuse, either for us or the dogs for which we are responsible.

Some people play viciously on their dogs' aggressive natures, encouraging them to attack and fight. They turn them into projections of their own sadism, a crime against both the victims of the violence and the animals themselves.

Dogs, like us, need laws and rules to protect us from what may lie less far beneath our skin than we like to think. Just rules, fairly administered, are a mercy both for us and for our dogs.

Walks in nature with my dog

Momentarily bored, he sits beside me, and we stare together at the gleaming moon

Dogs don't like to miss out. It's one of the upsides of refusing to take life lying down, unless they're just too comfortable, or, sadly, too old. Unlike most humans who walk up the street staring at their iPhones, they see, hear and smell what's in front of their noses. They notice, and help their humans to notice too. 'Life without wonder is not worth living,' said Abraham Joshua Heschel. It's a quality which dogs inspire, and I sometimes think of my walks with them as prayers, full of discoveries and meditations which leave my whole being, body and soul, more alert.

Jewish tradition mandates prayer three times every weekday: first thing in the morning, during the afternoon, and after dusk, with a further short reflection on going to bed at night. My dogs have accompanied and inspired me in all these liturgical obligations. They may not know the words of the prayers, though the sad yawn and bored resignation with which he lays himself down when he hears the opening Hebrew words suggest that Mitzpah has at least acquired some sense of what is liable to follow. What the dogs do understand, though, is the importance of noticing and appreciating the world, and there is surely nothing more central to prayer than the awareness of our blessings and the expression of gratitude.

It's a cold March morning in the Lee Valley. It's still early, but the strong sun has already melted the tiny white crystals off the frozen grass and small beads of water shimmer on the sides of the blades. We take the road through a village until we find a footpath and follow it out into the country. Soon Mitzpah is running free across the fields, racing over the shadows cast by the leafless trees. He bounds and chases in circles of visceral delight and his joy transforms my spirit. We cross wooden bridges over small rivers, the water flowing brisk and high. There are no other people around so I feel free to chant the morning service out loud.

I look up and realise that the dog has vanished: 'Mitzpah,' I call. 'Mitzpah, where've you gone?' Then I spy his snout, sticking out from the inside of the hollowed-out trunk of a dead tree.

'I'm hiding, I bet you can't see me,' he seems to be saying, before taking delight – like a happy child – in jumping out in front of me as if to cry, 'Here I am.' A mystic once explained to a person experiencing existential doubt that God is just like someone playing hide-and-seek. 'Look for me,' God says to humankind. 'I'm hiding everywhere, in the beauty of the trees, in the fierce magnificence of the sea and in the human heart.' What makes God weep is when we despair of looking.

The dog may not have given me my eyes, but he takes me to places where I see. We pass a hedgerow of hazel, elder and wild rose, the young buds on the cusp of opening. Through their intertwined branches, I note a small orchard of apple trees, and in the grass beneath them hundreds of daffodils. Mitzpah spins and dances in ovals and figures of eight, criss-crossing the path ahead. A blackbird hops away into the tangled vines of honeysuckle which weave themselves through the hedge. The phrases of the liturgy flow through my mind like a singing stream: 'The earth is full of what is yours God', and this morning the dog has taken me out to enjoy it. I think of how the mystics play on those words, like a dog joyfully twisting a rope this way and that, as if to see which shape is most pleasing. 'The earth is full of ways of finding you,' they explain, because there is nothing on earth which does not contain the secret, sacred energy of the divine life, and this bright morning one of those ways of discovering it consists in following the black and white tail of an eager hound.

I'm woken from my transcendent reverie by a flock of sheep on the run: why, I wonder, are they heading so swiftly towards that ominously open gate? 'Mitzpah,' I call in a flash of awareness, 'Mitzpah! Come here at once!'

'What?' he seems to say, 'Who? Me?' as, for once obedient, he mercifully sprints back to my side. 'I can't think why those stupid sheep could possibly have gone off in that direction.'

It's evening and we're in the New Forest. These wooded domains belong to a different universe from London; theirs is a world which moves at the speed of ponies pausing in the middle of the narrow road to chew – with what seems to city drivers like calculated slowness – a twig of yellow-flowered gorse; a world traversed by the fleet, silent deer; a world where the air smells of moor breath and moss breath, oak breath and pine breath, and wood smoke from cottage fires. 'Come on Mitzpah,' I call, but he's already squeezed past my legs and off along the path towards the gate which leads into the woods.

The dog looks back at me to check which way we're going. This time we don't cross the stream by the narrow plank to take the track towards the village green. Instead, we turn towards the forest, following the muddy path which ascends among the firs and beeches. The dog races ahead; I walk slowly, guided by the rhythm of my prayers. Each morning, before the rest of the family is awake, and almost every evening, I come to meditate with the trees. Mitzpah soon senses this liturgical impediment to his exuberance. He turns, half disappointed, to sniffing at the fallen branches, until the proximity of a careless squirrel persuades him that he shouldn't ignore the cheek of such deliberate provocation. He chases its rapidly retreating tail before halting with a four-pawed skid at the foot of a grey trunk, where, bouncing and barking with frustration, he stares upwards into the canopy in which the daring rodent has wisely disappeared. 'You can't climb trees,' I remind him, as he wanders back off to resume his survey of the latest canine news, reading the most recent posts from the root work of the trees.

Then, momentarily bored, he sits beside me, and we stare together at the gleaming moon. I begin the evening prayers in praise of the one 'who sets the stars in order in their watches in the sky'. Later that night, when the cold has gripped the mud and frozen it into gleaming furrows, my daughter Kadya joins us and tells us the names of the nearest constellations.

Back home in London, night walks are my favourite, setting off at last light on long summer days to join other late walkers and dog-minders around the heath. An owl cries from the dark line of trees which edge the fields. The ponds are without ripples as we run along the path that borders their banks, their stillness undisturbed by the late wind or the thrust of webbed duck feet. Bats fly cunningly around us; no fishermen are out this night. The whole world is ours to inhale. Beyond, to the south, are the blocks and skyscrapers of London, the Gherkin, the Shard, the Post Office Tower; so quiet from this distance, so full of countless lives, so vulnerable, and beautiful. But Mitzpah has no time to stop and stare; he's halfway up the hill and I'm forced to accelerate the easy, meditative pace of my running, steady my breath, shorten my stride and strive, a hopeless task, to catch him up.

Nachman of Breslav, the great Hasidic storyteller, loved the night-time too, though probably not in the company of dogs. Night is the time for refining the spirit, for meditation and purification, he taught, basing his reflections on the beautiful verse from Psalm 77, 'I call to remembrance my song in the night':

At night – because this is the time of the visitation of spirits . . . the principal time for contemplation, for being alone with oneself and one's Creator. This is the time to pour out one's speech before the blessed God, and converse with one's heart.

Back home, I give Mitzpah the chewy bar which is supposed to clean his teeth. Sensible dogs eat it slowly; Mitzpah devours it in seconds. I've never quite developed the habit of cleaning his teeth. On those rare occasions when I do approach him with that suspicious little brush spread with chicken-flavoured toothpaste, he promptly crawls beneath the table. It's generally unwise to accompany him into this 'personal' space, but, if I nevertheless dare to do so, he doesn't seriously object, even when I push apart his gums and polish his over-yellow teeth, promising myself that I'll be less neglectful in the future and that one day I'll even try out dental floss.

He follows me upstairs, climbs the steps which, for some inexplicable reason, since we bought them for a different purpose entirely, we've left as a dog ladder to help him onto the bed (where he shouldn't, strictly speaking, be sleeping anyway), then stretches himself across its width and length with proprietorial abandon. Any subsequent human occupant who dares to push him aside risks a semi-conscious growl. I've cultivated the art of using the duvet to flip him over; it's a necessity during those cold hours when I'm last to bed and find that he's left me a meagre six inches at the edge of the mattress and even less of the blankets.

I put one hand over my own eyes to prevent distraction, as Jewish custom demands; I place my other hand over the dog's eyes, about which Jewish custom says nothing, and recite the words of the meditation: 'Hear

O Israel, the Lord our God, the Lord is one.' I drift to sleep with the subsequent sentences fading into a slurring blur, 'and you shall love the Lord your God [or is it "the lord your dog"] with all your heart, with all your soul and with all your might.'

Mitzpah sleeps the perfect sleep of one who knows himself indulged. Only, occasionally, his paws move back and forth, as if he were reliving in his dreams the pursuit of an unfortunate squirrel or some eager race across the beach to reach the unfurling waves.

7
Asking

Dogs make full use of their eloquence when they sense even the
faintest indication that one is about to go out for a walk

No doubt there's much they're unable to inform us
about, but dogs are undeniably good at asking, especially when it's for food. It's hard to avoid the suspicion
that they practise their looks in the mirror: how else could
they have developed such inveigling skills of persuasion?
I've met people who know how to resist the mournful
beseeching of a dog's brown eyes, but I'm not one of them.

There's something about the very absence of language
which makes a dog's pleading even more eloquent.

It's harder to reprove the blessed beast for petulance, impossible to rebuke it for the failure to say 'please'. I'm not much of a fan of those small dogs that bounce up and down on their back legs like overenthusiastic trampolinists. It's the still, steady stare of the steadfast eyes to which I'm susceptible; the long, sad mouth and the big, attentive ears, the face which says: 'You do love me, don't you? Then how can you say no?'

Fundraisers would do well to pay attention; there's much to be learnt from canine skills in the persuasive arts. Dogs would be wonderful practitioners themselves if only they knew how to ask on behalf of others as well as they do for themselves, and understood the art of refusing the first offer and holding out for the largest contribution.

There's also much to be learnt from what dogs never ask. They don't pester you for gifts they don't want. They have no interest in showing off to their neighbours, in keeping up with Rover and Buster next door. They have no taste for upmarket trainers, fashion accessories or the coolest collar or basket. It makes no difference to them whether they sleep on an old rug or a posh duvet, so long as they feel close to those they love. They don't demand the latest electronic device, and have no need to be transported in the most up-to-date car. They don't want iPhones or earphones, don't care for podcasts or downloads, and are not obsessed with selfie sticks. They never ask for anything they don't really need, except perhaps for too much or unhealthy food. When they die, the lead hanging unused in the cupboard and the empty bowl and basket tell a sorrowful but simple tale. It's not what they own that counts, but the love.

Only once was Safi given an unnecessary accessory. Actually, it was a piece of ritual rather than luxury clothing, a garment with the eight-threaded tassels on the corners as the Bible enjoins. The dog was unimpressed with the vestment, and promptly raised a leg over one of the dangling fringes. Perhaps he wanted to show his awareness that even the strictest of rabbis never considered dogs included in the obligation to don such an item.

On another occasion, I bought Safi socks to protect a pad which had a sore. 'A fool and his money are easily parted,' observed Nicky, as the obvious became apparent even to me, that there was no way the animal was going to tolerate being clad in such ridiculous gear. The dog wellies we were given by someone who no doubt followed the well-meaning but mistaken view that it's really the thought that counts were equally quickly relegated to the bag containing all those objects which one knows one has to give away, but never quite dares.

In my experience, there are two main kinds of situations in which dogs make full use of their eloquence. The first is at the table, the second when they sense even the faintest, feeblest indication that one is about to go out for a walk.

Music may be the food of love for humans, but for

dogs the food of love is . . . food. So what can possibly be wrong with expecting, if not an equal portion to that of the human members of the clan, at least a modest share, a tiny taste? After all, if you don't ask, you won't get. Wisdom no doubt consists in never feeding one's dog at the table. Perhaps that's why Jewish law stipulates that domestic animals must always be fed first, before their humans sit down to dinner. The ruling is based on the saying in the Book of Proverbs that righteous people understand the needs of their animals. Sadly, my score comes out low in both righteousness and wisdom. Mitzpah, and Safi before him, have both made a fool of me. I do give in to their pleading, my excuse being that what I imagine Mitzpah wants is not the food but the message which it conveys: that he's truly part of the family. I do however keep a watchful eye on his weight and only ever give him a modest piece of something savoury, because it isn't the amount but the meaning that matters.

I stop short of cooking special dinners for the dog, let alone taking him to dog restaurants, if any exist in London. I once heard an interview with a diner, or rather the owner of a diner, when such an establishment first opened its doors to the canine public of Los Angeles. 'It's not just the menu my Pekinese enjoys; I bring her for the social,' the lady said. Whose social?, I remember thinking at the time, and my views haven't changed.

Even more difficult to resist than their pleas for food is the way dogs beg to be taken with you when they sense you're planning to go out. It's fine if you do intend to let them come. The moment they see you take the definitive action, by picking up a couple of extra poo-bags, by heading in the general direction of the cupboard which contains their lead, or by inadvertently mentioning the 'w' word, let alone by calling their name, an exuberant enthusiasm seizes their entire body.

'It's all right,' I say to Mitzpah as he observes me with dubious anxiety, while still refraining from removing himself from his warm corner on the kitchen sofa lest such an early morning effort should end in disappoint-ment, 'I'm not going anywhere without you.' Reassured, more by my movements than by my words, he draws his full length carefully down, stretches his back, takes a quick look behind him as if to make sure that his tail is actually following him, and heads swiftly for the front door. 'Let's go,' I say, in response to Mitzpah's ques-tioning glance as we head happily for the door.

'Yes, yes, yes, he's taking me with him,' he barks with exuberant impatience, annoying the entire household. I guess it's the canine equivalent of 'thank you', with an added 'do hurry up'.

Safi used to divide his ritual of persuasion into three distinct stages. It was my father who understood this best after caring for the animal while we were on holiday abroad. He liked to have a rest in the afternoon; Safi approved, so long as it didn't go on for too long and was followed by a trip up the road. My father explained: 'First he sits down and just looks at you. Then he comes nearer and licks your face. Finally, he scratches at you with his paw. So you might as well get up when he comes to look.'

Sometimes, though, there really is no choice but to leave the dog behind. 'Sorry Mitzpah, I just can't take you today. It's a long and boring meeting and there won't be time for a walk.'

He responds with a sad, unblinking stare: 'How can you be so cruel?' Occasionally he inveigles me into changing my mind, against my better judgement.

'OK then, but we'll have to work out where I can leave you.' He doesn't care about the qualifications; he knows he's won. That's how he came to accompany me to the BBC to record *Prayer for the Day*.

'We have to do a risk assessment before we can let him in,' I was told at the security desk.

'Risk assessment?' I asked, puzzled. 'Precisely what kind of threat might the animal pose?'

'In case', I was informed, 'he pees against the electric circuitry and sets the place on fire.'

Worst of all is when dogs spy a telltale suitcase. It's useless trying to reassure them by telling them you won't be away for long. 'It's all right,' I try, seeing his desperate look. 'We'll be back the day after tomorrow and the children will look after you.'

'You're breaking my heart,' he replies, his tail fallen, his posture shrunken, as he settles down in sorrowful resignation, staring at me with the meek mien of faithfulness betrayed.

For, of all the things dogs ask, the most important, more than food and more than walks, is love. It's the question implicit in their gaze from a thousand cages in rescue homes across the world. Will you take me with you? Will you love me? Will you give me a new home? In his disturbing film *City of Dogs*, set largely in the slums of Los Angeles, Louis Theroux comments sadly that dogs are a species human beings first colonised and then betrayed. Our treachery stares back at us from thousands of pained and pining eyes. They accuse; until, at whatever rate and after whatever span of time each particular shelter stipulates, they are put to sleep, their neglected lives brought to an untimely end, their potential for love sent unrequited into the eternal silence.

Perhaps, then, there are things for which dogs and other animals ought to be asking. No doubt they do, but we fail to understand, or choose not to comprehend. Or maybe the animals around us have a better measure of us than we like to think. I don't know if the accusation was real, or if it was only my projection, but on one vivid occasion I felt I was being cross-examined by a cow. It happened as I was walking down a lane by a field on a remote western promontory in the Scottish

Highlands. The cow lifted her head up from her grazing and caught me, I think deliberately, in her unyielding gaze. I stayed my pace and stopped, feeling myself interrogated by her challenging stare. I experienced an immediate sense of guilt. 'Yes,' I heard myself saying back in silence, 'I admit it. I do belong to that species which slaughters and eats yours.' But still the cow kept staring, and I stood still, chastened, feeling that to walk away would be a form of evasion, a denial of how cruelly we treat other sentient beings. To this day, the memory of that interaction is accompanied in my mind by a sense of shame. I've long been a vegetarian, an abhorrer of our brutal trade in the lives of our fellow creatures.

The philosopher Hans Jonas was awarded the Premio Nonino for the best book translated into Italian during 1992. It was expected that he would devote his acceptance speech to the subject of the Holocaust, in which his mother was murdered and which formed the background to his understanding of the centrality of ethics. Instead, he spoke of a concern which, he said, made racism look as petty, anachronistic and irrelevant as it truly was. The issue was the earth itself, a matter which called for universal human solidarity and responsibility. The latest revelation, he concluded, was not from Mount Sinai, Gethsemane or under a Bo tree; it was from nature itself, neglected and betrayed. It was 'the outcry of mute things' calling on us to curb our powers over creation, lest we perish together on a wasteland. After receiving the prize, he returned to New York where, three days later, he died.

Dogs, the actor and animal-rights campaigner Peter Egan told me, were the gateway: trying to see life through their eyes, he understood that he was being challenged to change his attitude not only to them but to all animal life and the whole of creation.

8
Listening

A dog can't tell you how he's feeling.
You have to learn to understand.

D og lovers often claim that their beloved animals understand every word they say. I'm inclined to agree with those who consider this a sentimental exaggeration. It's far more likely that our speech sounds to our pets like an unending sequence of *blah*, interspersed with occasional significant terms like 'walk', 'food', or their own name, though some dogs possess a considerably more extensive vocabulary than others. On that note, it's worth considering in advance what words one wants them to learn. Family legend tells of the woman who came to regret that she had taught her dog to do his business whenever she said 'empty', a term which, as she soon realised, occurs rather frequently in casual conversation.

Dogs probably think people talk far too much. They would agree with Shakespeare that, brevity being the soul of wit, humans could tighten up their act and give peace and quiet more of a chance.

Mitzpah has a particularly dim view of classical Hebrew. Boredom overcomes him as soon as he hears the first liturgical phrase in the sacred tongue. Realising that attention has veered away from him, he opts for the oblivion of sleep.

What dogs do comprehend, however, is a great deal of what we don't say. About this there is nothing sentimental; on the contrary, it can be acutely uncomfortable. They have a far finer ear than many of their two-legged companions for the feelings behind the words. It's charming when they discern the affectionate tone in a barrage of indecipherable endearments. But it's deeply disconcerting when they show that they understand us more acutely than we know ourselves. I've seen Mitzpah lower his tail and creep slowly out of my room, as if he were anxious to escape some undisclosed trouble before its eruption. Watching him sneak surreptitiously away, I realise that he's become aware, before I'm willing to acknowledge it myself, that I'm angry. He wants to make his getaway before it's too late. 'Don't engage with people in the moment of their anger' runs a perceptive rabbinic saying. Mitzpah knows this instinctively; I watch him go and feel ashamed. It's not a sign of grace when animals flee our presence.

We all communicate far more than the words we actually say. The very quality of our presence makes an impact. Maybe our consciousness emits certain kinds of vibration according to our varying moods: perhaps our different emotions also have their own distinctive odour. Sometimes I feel that even the trees understand us by means of invisible signals as we pass them by. Dogs certainly do. It's a chastening realisation.

Rachel Bluwstein, one of the first modern Hebrew poets, contracted tuberculosis while trapped in Russia during the First World War. After her return to Palestine, illness confined her life to an ever-diminishing radius of activity. No longer allowed to teach children, separated by her failing health from the hills and fields of the Galilee she loved, not physically fit enough to paint, she was eventually limited to a single room in which she wrote a sequence of profoundly moving poems. Loneliness made her especially sensitive to the unspoken. In one of her final compositions, addressed both to the man she had once loved and to people in general, she wrote: 'Will you hear my silence/You, who did not hear my words?'

It's a question I often ask myself as I try to listen to

the quietness, to the unstated thoughts between sentences. When I go to the home of a family in mourning, or when someone in pain comes to see me, I tell myself: be as present as possible; make yourself as small as possible. The kabbalists coined the term *tzimtzum*, contraction. Though generally used in a metaphysical context to describe how the infinite God created a finite world, it can also be used of the human self. To me it means silencing my thoughts, disciplining myself to ignore distractions and enabling my heart to be alert to the unvoiced feelings within and beyond the words which are spoken. I frequently fail. Dogs, it seems to me, often succeed. They have a natural aptitude for perceiving our heart's aches, even before we 'give sorrow words'. Safi would frequently come to my side before I said his name. Often when I wake up anxious in the night, Mitzpah crawls further up the bed, sniffing at me in sympathetic concern. They understand; they care.

Maybe that's why children like to talk to their dogs. A friend told me how worried she was now that the family dog was getting old: what would her daughter do when the beloved animal died? 'She comes home from school, sits down next to him and tells everything into his ear. Who's she going to confide in when the dog's no longer here?'

Reading dogs are a major hit in schools, not because, wonderful as they are, they've learnt to appreciate *A Bear Called Paddington* or *Winnie the Pooh*, but because, for young children, reading to a dog feels safe and unthreatening. Dogs won't interrupt, don't correct and never make them feel stupid. They help the children learn not only to decode the letters on the page but to understand the meaning of true attentiveness.

Not, of course, that dogs don't also fail: a fox stalks through the garden and Mitzpah races off barking like a maniac, or he gets bored and wanders away with a nonchalant lack of interest which most human beings have the decency at least to try to disguise. But, as often as not, dogs do stay and listen. Both Safi and Mitzpah spent innumerable hours next to the sofa, underneath the table, or at the feet of a visitor in tears. They had two advantages over humans. Firstly, their confidentiality was beyond question. I've occasionally thought what a disaster it would be if the dogs were to learn to talk, given the innumerable conversations they've overheard, patiently listening to the tribulations of a thousand lives. How much would people be prepared to pay for their silence? Secondly, they never put their paw in it by saying the wrong thing. They offer neither trite advice nor unhelpful platitudes.

There exists no stethoscope to place against the ribcage of another being to hear the unspoken language of its heart, except a listening heart of one's own. I would like to be as devoted a listener as a dog at its best.

But listening is a two-way process. Why should dogs

listen to us if we never listen to them? Dogs depend on us to do something harder than hearing their words, or barks, or growls or cries. We have to listen to their silences too. We can't even know how often dogs feel misunderstood or totally unheard. In the mixed-species families of which they often form such a loving part, they are almost always in the minority, the outsider whose language no one shares, whose signals no human adequately comprehends. Soon after Safi joined our family a friend took me aside and said, 'You know, having a dog is in some ways an even greater responsibility than having children.'

'Why?' I asked, puzzled.

'Because a dog can't tell you how he's feeling. You have to learn to understand.'

9
Healing

Dogs know how to cure with their
patient presence

Unlike most hospices, hospitals don't generally allow dogs to visit, for understandable reasons of hygiene. But there are exceptions, both planned and unintended. I remember seeing a news item about a family who were given permission to bring the dog to the hospital to say a last goodbye to their father who'd been in a coma for over a week. The dog barked, the man woke up, was declared fit shortly afterwards and went home to resume his normal life. One hopes his spouse was grateful.

More daring, though regrettably without the same results, was the feat of one of my congregants whose mother lay ill in hospital for several months before she died. Among her nearest and dearest were her two beloved dachshunds. Her son hid one of them inside a pillowcase and smuggled him onto the ward to visit his mistress. 'We think the nurses did notice,' he admitted afterwards, 'because not many pillows have a tail hanging out. But they kindly turned a blind eye.' Much as visiting the sick is regarded as a mitzvah, a good deed commanded by God, it is to the best of my knowledge not incumbent upon dogs, so I can't officially recommend my community to imitate such a deception, even though it gave the dying lady so much comfort.

Dogs would make excellent hospital visitors, though, and some are indeed trained through the charity Pets as Therapy (PAT) to do just that. From time to time I meet remarkable humans, humble and compassionate men and women, with an intuitive gift for caring for others with no expectation of reward. They sit quietly by the side of a sick person hour by hour; they know instinctively how to hold a cup of tea so that an elderly man whose hands tremble involuntarily can drink it without the liquid spilling. They don't look with begrudging impatience at their smartphone to see how long they've already spent in such duties, or how much longer it will be before another relative or carer comes to liberate them from their burdensome task. They understand that what matters most is simply and solely the bond of attentive, loving kindness. I think that many dogs know how to love like that, in steadfast, selfless patience.

Of all the many ways in which dogs assist us and bring us healing, it is probably guiding blind people which is the most ancient and best-known. 'You and I have both got guests tonight,' I informed Mitzpah recently, as if this early warning might somehow help him to prepare for the forthcoming canine invasion of his personal space. 'Berachah's joining us for dinner, with her guide dog, Dinka.' I had anxious visions of this noble helping hound being assaulted by the rabbi's dog on the holy Sabbath eve when the duty of hospitality is doubly sacred. In the event, I need not have feared; Dinka proved a relaxed and gentle guest who made herself sufficiently at home to drink from her host's bowl, while Mitzpah conducted himself with impeccable civility, as was not invariably his wont.

One day there will be electronic instruments to provide those who are visually impaired with all the data necessary for the safe navigation of every hazard. These sophisticated aids won't need lengthy and expensive training, or feeding, brushing and taking to the vet, or time of their own for daily recreation. Instead, all that will be required will be to attach the device to the arm or fix it to one's belt. No doubt such implements are currently under development. But, though they may restore the same degree, or more, of spatial awareness, they will never match a dog's capacity to bring light and brightness back to the heart. No machine can give love, the essential component in so many forms of healing.

Today there are numerous ways in which dogs help their humans, and affection is always a key part of their armamentarium. Medical Alert Assistance Dogs are taught to warn a person suffering from diabetes of an imminent high or low in their blood sugar. In this way, they often restore not just the individual but also their entire family to a reasonably normal life. It was 'a devastating shock' for them all when Jayne and Bill's one-year-old son Archie was diagnosed with diabetes. Every night he would have a hypo; for years, none of them got more than a few meagre hours of snatched and broken sleep. But when Domino, a beautiful young Labrador, came to join them after completing his training with Medical Detection Dogs to alert his young charge's parents whenever his blood sugar was rising or falling to dangerous levels, the family's life was transformed. With Domino by his side, Archie was no longer afraid to go to sleep for fear that he would never again wake up. 'Before Domino we were in a void, we never knew where to turn, we were unsettled. He has brought sunshine into our lives,' Archie's parents said.

Cancer Detection Dogs learn to recognise the possible presence of cancer, especially prostate cancer, through its distinctive smell in urine or breath samples. This greatly improves the chances of early detection, substantially increasing the likelihood of a good outcome. One dog even received a specially addressed postcard from a man who, thanks to the dog, was operated on in good time. It read simply: 'Thank you for saving my life.' The organisation's magazine is called *The Sniff*; there can't be many sniffs which can make the difference between life and death.

At Canine Partners, dogs learn to assist disabled people. At their training centre in West Sussex, I watched a dog being taught how to open and unload a washing machine. First, she learnt how to push the latch which released the door, then she carefully transferred the clean, freshly rinsed items from the drum to the hands of her trainer. I wondered if she was even going to manage to pair the socks, the ultimate domestic chore. With each successful manoeuvre she received praises, a treat and a cuddle. If more children were greeted with the same affectionate appreciation for every task well done, both home and school would be better-tempered places.

A second dog was being prepared for her partnership with a woman in a wheelchair. He was currently learning how to help her get ready for bed. He dexterously undid the Velcro fasteners on her shoes, tugged gently at the heels to free the items from her feet, picked them up in his mouth and handed them to her to put away. He, too, received a treat and a hug. It was obvious that both future owner and dog were thoroughly enjoying the whole process.

I don't think there are any dogs in the Bible which offer such immediate physical assistance. But there are different types and depths of seeing and hearing. In biblical Hebrew 'to see' often carries the wider meaning of becoming aware, of paying attention to the consequences of a situation. God 'sees that Leah is hated' when it becomes obvious that Jacob prefers her younger sister Rachel, the girl with whom he had fallen in love and intended to marry in the first place, had their father not deceived him. Later, Rachel 'sees' that she's borne Jacob no children, but that Leah has given birth to four sons, realising that what matters now at this later stage in their lives is no longer romance but providing their husband with offspring.

All kinds of dogs help many of us to 'see' in that symbolic way in which the Bible uses the term. I would often describe Safi as my therapy dog, and I frequently think of Mitzpah in a similar manner. They help to keep me sane, in their crazy ways. There are plenty of ills beyond the reach of conventional medicine which dogs know how to cure with their patient presence, a lick on the face, or their wise insistence that the world would feel better if we both went for a walk.

Sometimes it's not the pain or even the worry but the loneliness which hurts most. 'In the first terrible weeks after my husband was killed, I cried myself to sleep, then woke up again an hour later to find myself still crying', I once read. 'I would bang my head against the wall in hopelessness and anger. But still my dog slept next to me every night without fail, as if she understood.' The dog assuredly did; no doubt she comprehended something deeper than the gap on one side of the bed: the immeasurable empty space of pain, the urgent need for something tender to reinhabit the desolation of the heart.

There are yet further injuries which life can inflict on the soul – more complex and intractable, even less amenable to healing. Perhaps dogs also experience such hurts, though I'm sure they're incapable of causing them. These are profound child- or puppy-hood injuries, the result of cruelty, wilful neglect, contempt or abuse. People tell me things which leave me anguished and dismayed merely from hearing them. 'I was constantly told that no one loved me and no one ever would'; 'my father would tell me how he didn't want me; never had. He'd send me to my mother, who'd say the same'; 'the man took advantage of me; he used me time and time again. I felt powerless; that there was nothing I could do, that somehow this was the order of things. He made me feel dirty in a place I don't think I can ever clean. He made me hate myself, to this very day.'

There exists something even worse than depriving a person of love: to rob him or her of the feeling of being worthy of receiving love, of being lovable and capable of giving love at all. We are born with the capacity to respond to love; as it grows we develop the ability to love others in return. It is a sin to starve that faculty for love in another person, especially a child. It is an even greater sin to destroy the very capacity itself, to punch holes in the fragile membranes of the heart where those experiences are stored and garnered which nurture inside us the feeling that we ourselves are lovable, able to show kindness and capable of altruistic goodness. When that invisible faculty is attacked and mauled from childhood by careless or calculated cruelty, it is extraordinarily difficult to repair. The very vessel in which the healing liquids must be stowed in order to perform their work of inner restoration has been mutilated. Love offered later in life is liable simply to leak through it, like water from a bucket full of holes. One is left baffled and defeated in the desire to return to an innocent person his or her due feeling of self-worth. There can scarcely exist a greater form of betrayal than to damage another being in such a way.

Animals are not guilty of such treachery. They can be fierce, stealthy, cunning, remorseless, cruel. But they don't wilfully hurt for hurt's sake. They aren't vindictive; on the contrary, they share with the childhood victims of such cruelty a guileless innocence before the violent and duplicitous world of humankind.

That's why, in some circumstances, it's solely and precisely the love of an animal which can bring healing, self-acceptance, and the restoration of trust to a human being with an injured heart; trust, at least, in other animals if not in human beings. Dogs, with their loyal and unconditional affection, certainly understand the invisible art of enabling the tattered skin to begin to grow back over the bleak and bleeding inner spaces of the soul.

It was the gift of a German shepherd puppy which helped turn Sister Pauline Quinn's life around from a childhood in which she was threatened with death by a violent stepfather and repeatedly abused: 'It was the love of a dog that helped me to break down my own barriers,' she said. She felt safe and cared about for the first time; she learnt at last to trust. 'When I healed from my experience, I wanted to pass it on,' she wrote. She became a nun, joining the Order of the Dominicans, *domini canes*, the faithful dogs of the Lord, and devoted her life to helping refugees across the world. She persuaded hospitals in different countries to accept the victims of war and violence, and doctors to treat them for free.

The healing she received from a dog turned her into a courageous and indefatigable healer.

Round London in six
and a half days

Mitzpah soon realised he was the star of the show . . .
he proved a natural at looking straight into the camera

Mitzpah was part of the plan from the start; he was
two years old back then and full of cheekiness. The idea
was to walk round London in a week to raise funds for
the new synagogue my community was about to build.
Mitzpah was fitter, faster, more photogenic and far more
likely to gain sponsorship than I was.

It really all began when one of the children asked in
all innocence as we got into the car to visit my in-laws

who live in Kent, 'How long do you think it would take
to walk there?' We decided to find out. What was a drive
of a mere hour and a quarter proved to be a walk taking
three days. It was a wonderful family experience. A
highlight for me was going through the pedestrian under-
pass beneath the M25. When the dog ran through that
tunnel, I experienced a moment of deep exhilaration: it
felt as if for these few days we had defeated the mad
rush of cars and lorries and vindicated those most
ancient modes of transport, paws and feet. It felt similar
when we hiked as a family in the high Pyrenees, our
baggage carried by two donkeys. I thought they were
charming; other members of the family suggested
different adjectives. At one point Mitzpah was so tired
that he climbed into a parked car and made himself
comfortable on the rear seat. Unperturbed, the driver
asked us with a smile: 'Are your donkeys going to get
in too?'

Those walks provided the inspiration, alongside the
Bible. *Lech lecha*, 'Go walk,' says God to Abram at the
beginning of his great journey to find the Promised
Land. The mystics, noting that the literal translation of
the words is 'walk to yourself' understood the injunction
as an inner adventure too: walk until you discover who
you really are. How could I possibly find that out,
without the company of my dog?

Maybe that's also why it wasn't enough to undertake
any old walk: why should people sponsor us for that? I

determined to fix a route which would reflect my values and those of my congregation. That's how, on a series of cold March days marked by windy, wet and even snowy weather, Mitzpah found himself taken from hospital to hospice to care home, and from synagogue to church, mosque and temple, with further visits to Kew Gardens, the Woodland Trust's most recently planted forest, a reserve belonging to The Royal Society for the Protection of Birds, various interfaith organisations, the memorial to the Kindertransport on the forecourt of Liverpool Street Station, and even to Parliament, where he was sadly not allowed to accompany me inside. Perhaps it was felt that some of the people in there were already barking enough. Only guide dogs are admitted, notable among them David Blunkett's Lucy, the sole dog mentioned in Hansard, when the Prime Minister Tony Blair is cited as apologising for having accidentally stood on her tail.

We set out west as far as Kew, then followed the Thames on a blustery morning to the centre of town, before heading north and then west again to reach our furthest point at Theydon Bois. From there we curved towards home, stopping in St Albans, Bushey and finally, weary in body but not in spirit, back at our house in time for the forthcoming Sabbath.

I carefully arranged accommodation en route where the dog would also be welcome. Luckily, I couldn't find a single hotel willing to take Mitzpah, which saved us a fortune by obliging us to stay with friends. It proved to be a far more pleasant arrangement. I also tried to organise places to eat where the dog would not be excluded. This was not always possible. The website Styletails didn't exist back then, with its sympathetic blurb: 'You're out for a walk with your faithful friend and fancy a bite to eat, but where? Thankfully, more of London's restaurants are welcoming well-behaved dogs, some even catering for canines, with treats on hand for hungry hounds.'

At one point, I met up with a journalist friend to talk about the state of the world over lunch. Unhappy about leaving the poor dog outside in the rain, we finally despaired of finding anywhere that would let the three of us inside. We determined to ask no more questions but to smuggle the dog into the next eating establishment we encountered. To my surprise, we were entirely successful. We guided Mitzpah past the unsuspecting staff, prevented him from taking a passing lick at the sweet trolley, hid him under the mercifully large overhanging tablecloth, surreptitiously fed him the crusts of my toast, then, after paying the bill, led him back out into the street without a single person noticing.

Mostly, though, I munched my way through my meals on the hoof. Mitzpah soon realised that my bag contained items of considerable interest to a hound perennially eager for a little something extra. This brought an important benefit: all I had to do to bring him back to heel if he ran off too far was to slide the straps of my ruck-sack off my shoulders. He was at my side in an instant, eager to claim his fifty per cent of any bread or biscuits which might emerge from the generous pack.

Mitzpah and I shared the journey from beginning to end. Nicky accompanied me on two days, our daughter Libbi on one and a half, and our son Mossy on the last and weariest stretch. It was truly a shared endeavour; 'together' was our byword.

This was put to the test when we found ourselves next to a huge roundabout off the M25 at seven o'clock on an icy morning; even the dog was shivering. It was with huge relief that I spotted a large hotel a few hundred yards down a frost-whitened lane.

'Can I bring my dog in and have a cup of coffee?' I asked, and was happy to be welcomed inside. But while I was seated in the entirely empty salon waiting for my beverage, a waitress came over and informed me that she was 'terribly sorry, but we can't have dogs in here.'

'I did ask and was told it was fine,' I explained.

'I'm very sorry,' the lady repeated. 'Just leave your dog outdoors and come back for your coffee.'

'It's freezing out there,' I replied. 'Couldn't you kindly just bring me the drink; I promise to have it quickly and go.'

'I'm afraid we're not allowed.'

'We're in this walk together,' I said to Mitzpah, and together means together, I told myself, as I got up and left.

117

At the opposite side of the roundabout was a café used by truck drivers. Feeling equally cold and miserable, the dog and I made our way across the junctions to the wooden hut. 'Sorry love,' the lady at the counter said, 'you can't bring your dog inside, but why don't you both take a place in that corner in the covered area by the wall. It's sheltered from the wind and cold and I'll bring your coffee out with a slice of something hot for your dog as well.' The rules were the same, but not the attitude.

Mitzpah soon realised that he was the star of the show. The first photo opportunity came outside The Royal Free Hospital. I'd left the dog in a congregant's car while I was shown the latest medical technology in checking for bowel cancer, donated in memory of a beloved congregant who had tragically died from this cruel disease. Back outside, the team requested pictures. Perhaps it was because he was searching for the repeatedly mentioned cheese, but Mitzpah proved a natural at looking straight into the camera. He understood, too, that he had to be on best behaviour when we walked through the lobby and into the chapel at Great Ormond Street Hospital, where he had already attended on a number of previous occasions by special request of children on the wards. When we stopped off later the same day at The Three Faiths Forum, an organisation which works to build better relationships between people of different faiths and cultures, he again proved a perfect guest. I refused the grand armchair at the head of the group I had been invited to teach. Mitzpah, however, showed no such reticence. He climbed up, ate the vegetarian chewy bar specially provided for his delectation, and spent the dull half-hour of my lecture curled in refreshing repose.

The next day he mercifully refrained from chasing any birds at the RSPB reserve in Waltham Abbey. The following morning, he was as good as gold during assembly at a primary school in St Albans, where he demonstrated his few tricks with uncharacteristic obedience. Back in North London, on the final day of our adventures, he found himself warmly welcomed at The North London Hospice, where I noticed how several clients in the day-care lounge, one of them in a wheelchair, stretched out their hands towards him, finding solace in the warm touch of his fur. Our final visit was to a home for blind and disabled people, where he lay down on the carpet in the lounge and dozed to the music of the pre-Sabbath melodies.

When we returned home I had covered just over a hundred miles and Mitzpah at least three times as many, due to his habit of racing off in circles the moment I released him from the lead. The only times he refused to budge were during those stretches on which we had no option but to take the road. Hating the sound of traffic approaching from behind, he would simply freeze with fear until the offending vehicle had passed. 'Get him an iPod,' a congregant suggested. But what should it play? A general discussion ensued: maybe the sound of dogs barking in the distance, or perhaps the miaow of a fleeing cat? Sadly, the idea proved a non-starter; no kind of plugs would ever have fitted Mitzpah's oversized ears. I did my best to avoid stretches of road which made him feel vulnerable, but on one snowy evening I had no choice but to pick the terrified animal up. 'See,' I could feel him thinking, his paw curled comfortably round my neck and his head against my shoulder, 'I'm good at making this human do exactly what I like.'

We raised hundreds of pounds for every organisation we visited and several thousand for our new synagogue. Mitzpah earned his corner of carpet in my study, or rather in what, as I recently discovered, one family of congregants calls 'the dog room'. I also found out that I'd inadvertently been encouraging gambling, since it came to my attention that a number of worshippers were taking weekly bets on how many minutes of my sermon would pass before I first mentioned the dog. 'All right,' I said, aware that I would be unable to halt the practice, and that it offered the rare benefit of ensuring that they listened to at least the first portion of what I had to say, 'so long as the money goes to good causes.'

10
Rejection

We need each other, humans and dogs, and the whole,
interconnected, independent, infinitely vulnerable filigree of life

It was while browsing among the second-hand books
in a charity shop, with Safi lying bored at my feet,
that I found the children's story *Buster* by Linda Jennings,
with its sweet cover-picture of a dog looking sad and
the strapline on the back: 'Nobody wants me . . .' I
bought it at once. Buster is a much-indulged pet for
whom everything begins to go wrong when he grows
from being a gorgeous puppy into a proper dog. The
very same family who took him away from his mother

when he was just eight weeks old and called him cute and cuddly, now shout at him for chewing and playing, call him bad names and complain that he's nothing more than an irritating nuisance who always gets in the way. On 'one cold winter's day', they take him to a part of the town where he's never been before. They push him out of the car and leave him on a busy, noisy road.

The children listen, transfixed. 'That's exactly what happened to Safi,' we tell them. They are silent for a moment, then say together, 'But now he gets lots of love.'

Many dogs, and even more people, don't. A survey of stray dogs organised by the Dogs Trust showed that over forty-seven thousand dogs were abandoned across Britain in the year 2014–15. Despite all efforts to rehome them or keep them in safe kennels for life, on average at least one dog in the UK was put down every two hours.

'I was saved from the cruel streets of Sarajevo; please help me save my furry friends who aren't as lucky as me,' reads the caption next to the picture of a cute dog on the website of The Tanzie Project, which describes its mission as 'to bring awareness and support to saving the forgotten, displaced pets of Bosnia and Herzegovina, as well as in other areas of the Balkan Peninsula.' Sites from all over the world carry equally heart-rending pictures of dogs who long for a home.

It isn't only dogs. 'I sleep on buses if I've nowhere

else to go,' says a kind and dignified lady, currently a guest in our home, who's been a refugee in the UK for twelve harsh years. Innumerable people are persecuted in the country of their birth, forced to flee in terror for their lives, made to feel unwelcome in the lands through which they pass in search of refuge, and left feeling abandoned and rejected in the cities where they had hoped to create a safer, better future. Many are still children; before them should be life, hope, opportunity and excitement, not misery and alienation. I stood one day on the island of Lesbos during the months when refugees were daring the dangerous crossing from Turkey in thin, inflatable dinghies, some drowning on the way. I watched mothers arrive with their babies and small children and wondered: will there be somewhere in the world to offer a loving place for these people so utterly at the mercy of everything humanity and the elements cast against them? Nearby, a litter of six-week-old puppies played on the verge of the road. It was hard to know who was more unwanted.

In *City of Dogs*, his disturbing programme about life for dogs in Los Angeles, Louis Theroux captures the heartache of those in charge of the dog pound who find themselves with no choice but to make a daily list of which animals are going to be 'put to sleep'. He shows tough, streetwise men and women, no strangers to the harsh grind of inner-city poverty, weeping at the fate of these creatures. They allow him to film just one dog being led out on its final walk, but not to record the moment when the lethal injection is delivered.

During Safi's last days, when we realised with sorrow that we could not put off the painful decision much longer, we all took our moment to say our last words, deaf as he was, into his beautiful furry black ears. 'You've been a faithful dog,' I remember hearing Nicky tell him, and faithful he indeed always was, from the very first moment we led him into our home.

Faithful is probably the adjective most frequently associated with dogs; dogs epitomise faithfulness. Yet all too often we show little faithfulness towards them. From the long liturgy of confession on the fast of the Day of Atonement, one single expression always stands out for me: '*Bagadnu*, we have betrayed.' The word evokes in me an instant sense of shame: shame towards our fellow human beings left hungry, thirsty, cold, homeless, and sick; shame towards the wildlife whose homes we destroy; shame towards the domestic animals we treat like commodities, exploit and cause to suffer as if they were incapable of feeling. As Jeremy Bentham wrote in his essay, 'On the suffering of non-human animals': 'The question is not "Can they reason?" nor, "Can they talk?" but, "Can they suffer?"'

Centuries earlier, the great Jewish philosopher Maimonides had written in his *Guide for the Perplexed* that animals 'feel very great pain' when they see their young suffer, 'there being no difference in this regard between man and other animals'. 'The time will come', Jeremy Bentham concludes, 'when humanity will extend its mantle over everything that breathes.' The worry is, and so far the evidence has proved it, that this is not a mantle of compassion but of oppression. Intriguingly, the Hebrew word for clothing derives from the same root as the term for betrayal, presumably because both indicate concealment, in the one case benign, in the other out of deception and treachery. 'We have betrayed': I can think of no greater sin against the capacity for faithfulness and love so prevalent in so many dogs. Yet we need each other, humans and dogs, and birds and trees and fields, and the whole, interconnected, inter-dependent, infinitely vulnerable filigree of life. Only together can we survive on this planet; only with each other will we ever feel truly and fully at home on this earth. It is a devastating impoverishment of the spirit if it is never nourished by the wind's music in the trees; the sight of lambs, or calves, or puppies, the song of the birds at dawn and their sharp cries in the thickening air of dusk.

I fear for a world where animals are just a commodity. Though we won't want to admit it to ourselves, though we will refrain from putting it in such terms, in that world most of our fellow humans will be a commodity also, useful for this or that end. A friend who helped run a charity for protecting working animals against neglect and cruelty said to me candidly: 'It's often an issue which are the worst treated and the most exploited, the animals or the women; frequently it's the latter.'

No better will be a world where animals, and many people, are simply judged useless, not welcome here, not wanted in this country, or anywhere on the earth at all. How many people trying to sleep in the railway stations at night, in the freezing porticos and scarcely covered doorways of the central streets of our bleak cities, know that already in their cold and aching bones?

Another term from the Hebrew Bible comes to mind, the reflexive verb *lehitalem*, meaning 'to hide oneself away', 'to pretend one hasn't noticed'. 'Do not hide from your own flesh,' insists the prophet Isaiah. The distance between ignoring the needs of the animals who depend on us for all their requirements, including warmth and love, and turning a deliberately blind eye to our fellow human beings is small indeed. We live in a civilisation which all too often does both.

Dogs cannot formulate in words their response to the realisation that they are not wanted, that they are surplus to our requirement for their love. Instead, their pain stares out at us from their eyes, in looks of perplexity and unrequited longing, from which we walk away.

11
Forgiveness

Forgetting makes no demands on the heart, forgiving does; and dogs know how to forgive

Sadly, for many humans, today is haunted by yesterday and overshadowed by tomorrow. It's not easy to live fully and simply in the moment. Dogs, too, carry in their hearts the emotional impact of their past. But they have a gift for living each day free from the imaginations of a looming tomorrow with all its uncertainties and worries. They raise up their eyes unto the hills, they lift up their noses to the scents of the air; they know how to savour their 'now'.

I can say hand on heart that I've been good to my dogs. I would have a better conscience if I thought I'd behaved towards the humans I'm close to quite so consistently well. I once received a furious letter from a man who felt I hadn't done anything like enough to help him with a particular project in which I also had an interest. After detailing my various shortcomings, he concluded by informing me that I'd treated him incomparably worse than my dog. When I shared the missive with the chair of my community, he dismissed the rest of the contents out of hand, before adding with a smile, 'But, let's face it, the bit about the dog is true.'

Nevertheless, I've sometimes fallen short of being kind. I've spoken angry words because something else entirely has upset me; I've given an unwarranted tug on the lead to speed Mitzpah up because we're in a hurry, not because of him but because I left the house late; I've yelled at him because somebody has shouted at me; I've let out my bad temper, just because I'm in a bad temper – of all these sins I have been guilty.

Yet, come the evening, the dog is there to welcome me, jumping up with excitement, his tail wagging the rest of his body, his eyes full of love. Or I return from a work trip after three days, and there he is, sniffing my bags, my anorak, my shoes, wondering perhaps, 'Has he been out with any other dogs while I've been waiting here?' Or maybe he's checking to see if I've brought him back a present.

How can dogs be so forgiving? Some people say that it's because dogs are quick to forget. It's probably true that, unlike many humans, they don't bear grudges or harbour thoughts of revenge. I don't think dogs spend silent, vindictive hours determining how and when to retaliate. They don't rehearse to themselves every word or incident which ever upset them. They don't store away the past in the sour preservative of mental spleen. They don't embitter their own lives.

But I don't think it's because dogs are forgetful. It was Safi who first taught me what an excellent memory a dog can have. A few days after he joined our household I took some tablecloths to the dry-cleaner's in preparation for the Passover festival. For months afterwards, every time we passed that shop he would instinctively turn towards the door and pause to see if we were going to go in.

Bad memories make a particularly deep impression on a dog. Once we were walking along a nearby canal when a loud bang broke the silence, followed by another. I saw first one bird, then a second, stoop from the arc of its flight then fall like a stone from the sky. Near where they landed I spotted a man with a rifle. To this day, the dog hates to go anywhere near that place, beautiful though it is.

Worst of all are the memories of hurts experienced when dogs were just puppies. A friend told me how she adopted a dog with marks and scars on its back. Every time she or her companions made so much as to pick up a pail of water, the animal instantly fled. It had never forgotten the terror of being deliberately and cruelly scalded.

So it isn't because they lack the capacity for remembering that dogs have such an ability to forgive. Forgetting makes no demands on the heart, forgiving does; and dogs know how to forgive.

Forgiveness depends on seeing the value of a relationship as greater than the offence. The person who apologises says in effect, 'I recognise I've hurt you and I'm truly sorry. I take responsibility for what I did and mean never to do it again.' The person from whom forgiveness is sought doesn't have to respond with a cheerfully accepting, 'That's OK then; let's just carry on as if nothing ever happened.' Rather, by accepting the apology, he or she implicitly says, 'My relationship with you matters more to me than this hurtful incident. It did happen; what you've done has really hurt me. But because I appreciate that you understand why, and that you're really sorry, I'll try not to hold it against you any longer. Instead, we'll both learn from it, and it may even deepen the bond between us.' Forgiveness is about friendship and love being stronger than resentment. The greater the love in proportion to the hurt, the easier it is to forgive. Perhaps that's why, as Alexander Pope expressed so memorably in his aphorism, 'To err is human, to forgive divine', forgiveness ultimately belongs to the God of love, and to the loving part of ourselves.

I think it's because they have such a capacity for affection and devotion that dogs are so quick to forgive. It's because most dogs are so ready to be loving that they don't seem to hold onto grievances, while we – with our minds turning everything that happens to us round and round again – find it hard to let go of injuries and insults. Tellingly, the first half of the biblical verse containing the famous commandment to 'love your neighbour as yourself' teaches us 'not [to] seek vengeance or nurture a grudge'.

Perhaps, too, dogs have less to lose by being forgiving. Power often plays a significant role in the human tension over apology and forgiveness. We don't want to admit what we did wrong – to ourselves, let alone to anyone else – because it is painful to know that we are fallible and vulnerable. We don't want to appear weak before others, so we hold back from admitting what in the depth of our conscience we know to be true. But dogs don't seem to suffer from such pride. Perhaps we, too, find it easier to apologise to the dog because we don't have to humble ourselves, certainly not before anyone else. It costs little to look the dog we love in the eyes and say, 'I'm sorry I shouted at you this morning.' No doubt when we do so, we don't have floating in our mind such unpleasant thoughts as, 'She's going to gloat over me now' or, 'Who's he going to tell first that it was all my fault?'

Or maybe dogs and other animals are more in tune

with the great tides and movements of life, like the grey whales about which Eleanor O'Hanlon writes with such beauty in *Eyes of the Wild*. She describes how, even after centuries of persecution and killing by humans, mother whales – in those Californian seas where they know they are now protected – bring their babies close to the boats of the sightseers, encouraging the passengers to touch them. She acknowledges that there may be a pragmatic explanation for their conduct, such as an attraction to the sound of the outboard motors. But she clearly sides with those who believe that 'the whales' attitude and behaviour have a profound spiritual dimension: they reach out in a gesture of forgiveness for the suffering and death they have known at human hands'. Perhaps life itself desires to be forgiving.

Yet there are times when forgiveness feels wrong. It hurts to see a dog obey in cowed anxiety the bully who mistreats it. Just as human dignity itself is wronged when an abused woman feels forced to submit to a violent partner out of abject terror and the sense that she has nowhere to run to and no one she can tell, so vicious cruelty towards any living being is an offence against creation, against life itself, against God.

But when the dog comes running to the door and jumps up to greet me, even though I had no time for his walk that morning, or forgot to give him his break-fast, or shouted at him to get out from under my feet, he expresses a love which not only melts my heart but has much to tell me about how I, too, could be more generous and forgiving.

12
Consolation

With love on both sides, it's always
a healing and consoling partnership

The man was hunched forward in the chair in my
study. 'I just don't know what to do. I can't bear
my life any longer.' He stared silently down at his lap,
leaned forward and folded his arms tightly around his
head in an attitude of utter hopelessness. A moment
later the sound of his sobs filled the room and he began
to shake. I didn't know what to say: after all, what words
are there to sweeten the bitterness of such utter despair?
But, while I was stuck in the numbness of my silence,

Safi put his front paws on the man's lap and started to lick away his tears. I don't know if it was the shock of this unexpected therapeutic intervention, or the dog's obvious unconditional love, but the man looked up, his features softened, and for a moment the creases of pain eased from his cheeks. I think he may have smiled. I wouldn't even have known how to begin to offer comfort like that.

I, too, have been comforted in my tears by my dogs. I rarely cry in public. But at home, and often in secret, I sometimes find myself weeping, for my father, for my friends who've died too young, for the pain I witness almost daily, even here in a land at peace, far from the immediate landscapes of war and destitution. Yet here, also, we are not immune to terrorist attacks and to disasters, accidents and fires. New causes of fear have entered our streets and public gathering places and penetrated our hearts. They make us all the more aware of the significance of solidarity with each other, whatever our faith or station, and of our interconnectedness with all life. So my dog comes, and puts his head next to mine, and I weep all the more because life is weeping with me. And then I stop, and stroke the dog, as if his eyes and ears and soft fur represented all the tenderness that needs not just our tears, but our care and our affection.

Maybe that's why dogs are usually such welcome visitors at hospices. They bring their love with them and the touch of their fur is simpler than words. During the years when I was part of the chaplaincy team at my local hospice, I would observe how the dog was always included on a client's family tree. Often when I went to visit a patient in his or her room, the dog would be there, quietly keeping an affectionate watch. One lady told me how, while her husband was terminally ill, she took the dog to see him every day. The animal didn't beg for her usual long walks or bark like her habitual boisterous self when someone knocked on the door. Instead, she sat peacefully by the bed, watching steadfastly hour after hour. By then her husband was so weak that he rarely felt like speaking. But, the lady explained, from time to time he would reach down with his hand until it found the dog's head. He let it rest there, as if in a gesture of blessing, and the dog would look steadily up at him with full, unblinking eyes, as if she understood.

Dogs aren't good at words; instead they offer something deeper, something which too much language tends to obfuscate, a gift for transforming silence into love. Maybe that's what they understand, that all we really have is this now, this moment here, when all that truly matters is that life encounter life in loving kindness.

I once negotiated the special permission required for a friend's dog to accompany her into the cemetery when she visited her daughter's grave. 'Dogs aren't allowed here,' the superintendent explained, kindly but clearly. 'Some people might understand, especially if they were also dog-lovers; but most would think it inappropriate and worry about the mess the dogs might leave.' However, when I told him that the dog was both a mourner and a comforter at once, that the young girl buried here had held her as a puppy and chosen her name, and that the dog no doubt remembered, and that this shared memory was a unique source of solace to the girl's mother in her loss, he turned towards me and said with a quiet smile, 'I'll make an exception.' I realised then that he, too, was a man who knew from experience the unfathomable caverns of grief.

I almost always take my dog with me when I officiate at funerals; both Safi and Mitzpah have been frequent companions. Of course, I don't bring the animal into the chapel or take him to the graveside. That would hardly be fitting, though I did on one occasion honour the last wishes of a woman who asked me to arrange for the burial of the ashes of her seven beloved dogs on top of her coffin when she passed away. It's always a matter of knowing the right rabbi to ask.

I try to arrange my day so that I don't have to rush back home to my next appointment after a burial service. Instead, I take the dog for a walk. I watch him wander down the path between the trees, sniff among the leaves, sit waiting while I pause on a bench. Somehow, he helps me to reconnect with the rhythm and beauty of life; the measured, unending flow of vitality which brings the leaves to birth in spring and scatters them in the autumn wind, which makes the blue tits and the finches sing and the owls cry out at night, which gives me breath and animates my heart, until it, too, dies and is slowly, gradually refashioned by the transformative soil into fresh new life.

I have also, on occasion, though only by special request, brought the dog with me to houses of mourning. According to ancient Jewish custom, the immediate family of the deceased remain at home for seven days following the funeral, while the community takes care of all their needs, practical, emotional and spiritual, from cooking their meals to leading the memorial prayers. 'Where's Mitzpah?' a friend once asked me, days after the loss of his son. 'In the car,' I replied. 'Then bring him in!' Dubious but dutiful, I brought the dog inside, where he licked the hands of the family, which, though not exactly the traditional greeting to a mourner, was certainly warmer and more effective than the uncertain words of numerous two-legged comforters fearful of saying the wrong thing. Then he lay down at the father's feet to be stroked. A couple of weeks later I discovered that the family had got themselves a puppy, a ball of spinning, twisting, rolling, furry affection.

Looking back on those raw and frightening months, the bereaved parents told me a year later that it was the dog who had played a major part in getting them through that terrible first year. 'You can't face getting out of bed,' they said, 'but you have to, because of the puppy.

Consolation

You weep, and he comes and sits on your lap. You gaze into space with incomprehension, and he drops his toy at your feet and demands your attention. You don't want to go out, but he insists on his walk. You can't face other people, but they talk to the dog, and then you realise that you're talking to them too.'

Some years ago, I read about the experiences of a young woman during the first, impossible two years after she became a widow. Life was devastatingly lonely and unrelentingly painful. Everyone proffered advice, all with the best of intentions, none of it to any avail. Then someone asked her, 'Have you thought of getting a puppy?'

'What on earth for?' she responded, shaken for an instant out of the habituated numbness of her grief by sheer surprise. She'd never been a dog person; it was human, not animal, companionship she craved. Why a dog? The idea of a puppy hadn't even entered her mind.

The advice was ridiculous, irrelevant, absurd; but at least it was different from the usual well-intended ministrations. Without ever fully understanding why she did it, and entirely to her own surprise, she found herself following this unexpected counsel. She quickly discovered that the very people who had previously seemed to be avoiding her now stopped to talk to the puppy. First, they greeted the dog; then, via the subject of its breed, age, charms and needs, they began to talk to her. Friendships developed. Every park has its bands of dog walkers: the early morning runners trying to keep pace with their hounds, the midday strollers with their Pekinese and poodles, the take-the-dog-through-the-park-on-the-way-home-from-school-and-kill-two-birds-with-one-stone mothers, and the must-take-him-out-again-in-the-evening night crew. She no longer had that feeling of which so many bereaved people speak: the sense of walking down the street enveloped in the strange and muffling cloak of invisibility.

When people now tell me after a bereavement that they're considering acquiring a dog for companionship, I'm increasingly shameless about encouraging them to do so. I never, or so I pretend to myself, volunteer the idea out of thin air: it's hardly part of the traditional rabbinical brief. But when I hear someone say that they've been thinking about it for a while, I feel I have their permission. I firmly believe that, with love on both sides, it's always a healing and consoling partnership.

The Hebrew Bible has a remarkable idiom for giving comfort: 'speaking upon the heart'. Not everything that speaks upon the heart does so through the medium of human language. The loyalty of a dog, the lick of its tongue against a cheek, grey from tiredness and tears, can offer a consolation more eloquent than the greatest of well-intended speeches. 'I am with you in your troubles,' says God in the Psalms, and dogs have their way of saying the same thing. Only, unlike with God, who may indeed offer comfort in the secret recesses of the heart but can't be seen or felt, one can reach out a hand and touch the dog's ears, sit down and the dog sits next to you, stand up in quivering uncertainty, and the dog watches every move of every trembling limb in concentrated love.

What, though, if a new and different fear assails the heart? What will happen when the dog, too, dies? Even accepting comfort is a risk, like all love which softens and exposes the heart.

But we can't reject love, including the love of a dog, because one day it will be over. We carry in our heart not just the emptiness of their absence when those we love are dead, but also the fullness of all the companionship we were ever blessed to share. The people we love still speak to us from inside our mind. The dog who ran bounding in front of us still accompanies us in our affectionate reminiscence and blesses us from inside our heart. Death takes away the presence of the being we have loved, but not the love itself.

A walk up the Rhine

Mitzpah, tired after running his typical sixty kilometres,
had curled up for a rest on the cobbles

My longest walk with Mitzpah was a three-week
pilgrimage from Frankfurt back home to Finchley. We
followed the River Main to Mainz, turned north along
the banks of the Rhine, through vineyards and woodlands, passing the towns of Koblenz, Cologne, Bonn and
Duisburg, before crossing into Holland and, via a detour
to Amsterdam, heading for the North Sea shore and the
ferry back to England.

My reasons for undertaking this journey had nothing

to do with the dog. My community was building a new synagogue. But I've always associated worship with places that are old, the few venerable synagogues which still exist across Europe, not destroyed by the Nazis; small, thousand-year-old country churches. I wanted to find a way to enable our novice building to become a place of the spirit, imbued with the reverence and humility of prayer.

At the time, I was re-reading my grandfather's memoirs. He had served as a rabbi in Frankfurt from 1910 until he fled for his life in 1939. He wrote about how, on the morning after Kristallnacht, the Night of Broken Glass on 9–10 November 1938, when hundreds of Jewish premises were destroyed across Germany and tens of thousands of Jewish men arrested and many killed, he was summoned by the Gestapo to the central synagogue on the Börneplatz. There, he overheard people in the large crowd of bystanders saying that in the West End Synagogue, where he had frequently officiated, everything had been smashed yet the Eternal Light was still burning. The idea of a light that had proved inextinguishable, even amid the thickest moral and political darkness, spoke to me immediately. I determined there and then to go to Frankfurt, kindle a symbolic torch from its flame and bring it home to London to illumine our new Everlasting Light so that the flame of the past could burn in our fresh building.

It quickly became clear to me that if it was to have

any serious meaning, I had to undertake at least a significant part of this journey on foot and make it into a
pilgrimage, visiting Christian, Jewish and Muslim
communities on my way. If I was going to be walking,
how could I possibly go without my dog? Besides, his
companionship would make me feel safer should I ever
feel lonely or overwhelmed by the haunting history along
the route.

The first problem was how to get Mitzpah to Frankfurt.
Both he and Safi before him loved travelling by car. Both
had the gift of making themselves comfortable by
stretching across the full width of the rear seat, which
invariably bore the testimony of their affection in the
form of innumerable hairs and little lumps of mud.
Mitzpah had the additional habit, when he was small,
of snuggling his way through to the passenger seat, from
where he would either stick his nose through the inside
of the steering wheel or place his head on my lap in
such a way as to make it all but impossible to change
gear. Much as I loved him, this was a habit I had to
curtail in the interests of health and safety.

Both dogs also liked the train, in particular the
Caledonian sleeper, which once, or – if we were really
fortunate – twice each year carried our family to the
glorious Scottish Highlands. Both dogs understood when
we were about to take the sleeper and scrupulously lifted
their leg against every pillar along the platform. Then
they would clamber on board, march into our compart-

ment and waste no time before crawling underneath the bunks and promptly going to sleep, or, chancing the generosity of our holiday spirit, climbing up and making the lower bunk indivisibly their own. 'Look,' said Nicky, pointing at Mitzpah, 'the cheek of it; the brazen proprietorial ease.'

But on this occasion neither car nor train would serve. I had to be in London until the conclusion of the Sabbath before the start of our long walk, and in Frankfurt by eleven o'clock the next morning, when, as chance would have it, the centenary celebrations for what had formerly been my grandfather's synagogue were taking place. I had been invited to speak on what was sure to be an especially moving occasion for me, since my grandfather had been present at the dedication a century earlier and had addressed the congregation at the re-dedication after the Holocaust, in 1950. There was only one thing for it, to travel by plane.

I called the airline. The initial soundings were positive; there was indeed a flight at an appropriately unearthly hour that Sunday morning. 'Yes,' said the lady at the desk, 'we do take dogs.' 'No,' she continued in response to my next enquiry, 'we don't put them in the ordinary hold, but in a special heated area where they're comfortable and safe.' It sounded perfect; all I had to do was to bring the dog, with his up-to-date passport, of course, to the departures desk at the airport. How would I retrieve him after the flight? 'Perhaps,' a friend suggested helpfully, 'he'll come up on that escalator thing at baggage retrieval.'

I gave the matter no further thought until two weeks prior to leaving, when I decided I'd better double-check with the airline because it had all sounded too simple to be true and it would be a disaster if anything went wrong on the day. 'Of course,' I was informed on this occasion, 'you'll need an appropriate dog crate.' It was the first I'd heard of such an item. 'You can find the relevant sizes on the web.'

I was advised by a friend that there were three online services for people determined, or foolish, enough to take their dogs with them by air: High Dog, Fly Dog and Skydogs. (The information proved only partially correct: High Dog turned out to be a service offering counselling in case your dog accidentally got high.) I fail to remember which one we contacted, but the first question they asked was, 'Can we have your dog's vital statistics please?' These proved to consist of two measurements, the distance from the end of his nose to the tip of his tail and from the top of his ears to the ground. Mitzpah is by no means a very large dog; he's not especially tall and has maintained a slinky figure. But it was his length and the size of his ears that were his undoing, 'You'll need extra-large,' we were duly informed.

We set out in pursuit of such a crate, and were in fact on the verge of finding one, when other problems intervened. 'I'm afraid,' we were now informed by the airline, 'the combined weight of the crate and the dog will mean that he has to travel as freight.'

'What would that involve?' I enquired.

'Just drop him off at the airport on the Thursday before your departure date and we'll try and get him on the same flight as you, early on the Sunday morning, though we can't make any promises.' I don't remember if I said 'you must be crazy' out loud down the line, or if I managed to replace the receiver before giving vent to my feelings. Did the gentleman really imagine that I would leave the poor animal untended in some warehouse for up to three days, just in case he could travel on my flight?

It was only a few days before we were due to depart, and I needed an urgent solution to my problem. 'An alternative approach', a different website advised, 'is to pretend you're blind, in which case you are permitted to take the dog with you on board.' Underneath was a caveat: 'To the best of our knowledge this method has never been tried.' Or, possibly, the few who succeeded had wisely declined to record their triumph on the web.

In the end, a close friend drove with me through the night, chugging on the midnight Chunnel underneath the sea. Mitzpah lay in lazy comfort on precisely that section of the rear seat of the car which hadn't been covered with a towel to protect the upholstery against dog hairs. And, in case the journey should prove too lengthy for his bowel rhythms, or indeed for our own, we took him out for short walks at midnight, and again at two and four in the morning. He arrived in Frankfurt refreshed; we got there exhausted.

The walk was wonderful, a highlight of my life. I kept a blog, so that my community could travel with me virtually, and a dog-blog, aimed at children. I was soon informed however, that the animal's literary merits were rated well above my own.

Mitzpah shared both the blessings and the sorrows of the journey. There were moments of unanticipated kindness. On our very first day we stopped for a drink and a snack. 'Do you think your dog would like some bread?' the waiter asked me politely. In Germany, almost all cafés and restaurants were dog friendly. I told him that I assumed he would, whereupon the gentleman disappeared into the kitchen, emerging a moment later with a slice of baguette so thin and small in diameter that the dog didn't even have to chew to swallow it down. Back he went for a second slice, a third, and then a fourth, at which point I felt I ought to call a halt to the proceedings. When I made to pay, the man refused the money: 'Bread and water are the gifts of Jesus,' he said; he wouldn't dream of charging me for them.

The next day we were climbing in the hills above the Rhine when, as a type 2 diabetic, I realised my blood sugar was getting unhealthily low and that I had foolishly forgotten to bring any food with me. The only restaurant in sight was housed in a small and highly elegant castle. 'We aren't their kind of clientele,' I remarked to Mitzpah as I eyed the tables laid to perfection with four knives and forks on either side of each plate and several tall crystal glasses adorning each setting. But I had no choice, and asked the waiter if he kindly had any sandwiches. The man disappeared without a word. After a couple of minutes, I called to Mitzpah and, muttering, 'Fair enough, I thought so,' made to leave. But at that very moment the gentleman returned with a beautiful plate containing many kinds of fruit and different breads. Seeing me reach for my purse, he simply said 'for your pilgrimage' and smiled. I made sure Mitzpah received his fair share of the gift.

On one occasion Mitzpah did rather better than mere bread. While I was sitting writing up his blog on the veranda of a small restaurant where I'd stopped for a coffee, the waitress came out to ask me if she might offer him some dinner. It looked for all the world like raw pork sausage; but I could see no reason why I should be obliged to refuse. The food would go straight from the waitress's hands into the dog's mouth, without so much as a touch from his Jewish owner. Anyway, who was to say that dogs could only have kosher meat? I could see Mitzpah looking at me as if to say, 'You're not going to be a super-religious spoilsport, are you?' Indeed, I wasn't.

But not all the experiences were sweet. It was a route haunted by history, not just the utter destruction by Hitler of a thousand years of Jewish life along the Rhine, but also the devastation nine hundred years earlier wrought by the First Crusade. In the small town of Bingen, we were welcomed by a circle of non-Jewish citizens who explained what had happened during the terrible years of the Nazi persecution. 'I was a small child and remember seeing the flames when they burned down the synagogue,' an elderly man told us. 'Yes, and when the stone-carved lions over the entrance fell down and smashed they called out: "*So soll es sein*" – that's how it ought to be.'

They took us outside to where a group of three brass *Stolpersteine*, 'stumbling stones', were set in the cobbled pavement. I squatted down to read the inscriptions. 'That's exactly what the artist intended,' explained our hosts. 'The idea is that they should attract the attention of passers-by, who then stop to read.' Here had lived a family of three; the inscriptions provided their names, dates of birth, and the year when they were deported. They were all taken to Lublin in 1942. At the bottom of each of the stones, in size no more than five or six inches square, was a row of three question marks: where had this family perished? This, presumably, would never – could never – be known.

Mitzpah, tired after running his typical sixty kilometres to my more sedate mere twenty, had curled up for a rest on the cobbles. I recalled as I looked at him how the Nazis had required all Jewish families to surrender their pets alongside their radios, and any other possessions which might either offer the opportunity of keeping in touch with the wider world or provide solace and companionship. One account described how the animals intuitively understood; this was one walk on which they were instinctively unwilling to set out. Mitzpah looked miserable; I wondered if he somehow sensed the sorrowful history of this ordinary street.

He looked equally sad when on a grey afternoon we passed the Lorelei, the high rocky outcrop overlooking the sharp bend in the Rhine where, according to legend, a siren lured the enchanted mariners to their death in the fatal currents beneath. The Jewish poet Heinrich Heine had composed a ballad which was set to music and became so well known that even the Nazis, in their drive to purge German literature of all traces of Semitic pollution, couldn't stop people from singing it. They simply declared the song 'anonymous'. My grandparents used to speak about this; about how a people could be made to disappear from the culture, before it was physically killed off.

On one occasion, Mitzpah did receive his own come-uppance, his sole encounter with anti-Semitism. It occurred as we were walking through a small village. A cat sitting in a shop front took great offence at the notion of a dog passing safely beneath its gaze. She jumped, hissing, towards the window, showing Mitzpah her teeth and outstretched claws. Of all imaginable feline attire, she was wearing a cross on a chain around her neck.

This incident aside, we were met with almost universal friendliness to both dog and human. Mitzpah accompanied me everywhere; he came with me to interfaith panel discussions, cathedrals, synagogues and museums, behaving impeccably virtually the whole time. I was especially anxious when I was informed that a certain talk I had been invited to give was to be preceded by a special concert. I wasn't sure Mitzpah would take kindly to a violin solo, and the thought of it becoming an unintended duet was not one which I relished. In the event, he realised that on this occasion silence, at least on his part, was golden.

Perhaps the most significant moment in our companionship came when we reached the monastery of Maria Laach, where I had been invited to stay overnight and meet the monks. The dog and I were graciously asked to join the prior for dinner; yes, the dog was expected too. Mitzpah, whom I had taken care to feed beforehand, lay quietly on the carpet at our feet. Looking at him, my host observed how animals remind us that we humans are not the sole focus of creation. We are just a part of God's work, alongside all other living beings. In former days, pilgrims would arrive here with their donkeys or horses, which would be given hay and stabling while the men who led them found hospitality with the monks. Our separation from the animals, the prior continued, has led us to forget the bonds which unite us with other creatures. We should think of them not as pets but as companions on this earth, whom we are required by God to treat with respect and concern. Mitzpah, realising he had become the subject of our conversation, thumped his tail approvingly against the wooden floor. The prior's words, spoken with gentle kindness and total conviction, reminded me of the ancient saying by Rabbi Chanina son of Dosa: 'Those with whom their fellow *creatures* are comfortable, God is comfortable with too.' Sadly, it is usually translated as, 'Those with whom other *people* are comfortable . . .' I prefer to stick to the literal meaning of the original Hebrew noun *beriyot*, created beings, which includes the animals. They often know us more deeply than we know ourselves; their simplicity, if we pay them heed, can simplify and humble us too.

Mitzpah and I walked about 450 kilometres together, our route ending on a freezing, wet and stormy day at Hoek van Holland on the North Sea coast, where those children sent by their parents to safety in England on the Kindertransport in the final months before the start of the Second World War came through on their passage to safety. There was not sufficient time in the three weeks I took off from other commitments to cover the entire distance on foot. Mercifully the crew who filmed our pilgrimage had a car to which we had recourse whenever the day's distance was simply too great to cover by walking. Mitzpah grew fond of our companions, and of being filmed. On one occasion, he demonstrated his familiarity with the camera by running straight at it and knocking it flying.

Of course, I took him with me to the premiere. He sat patiently on the cinema floor for the first half-hour, but then, hearing loud barking from the front of the hall, he felt himself called upon to reply in full voice. The entire audience burst into laughter.

13
Trust

'I trust life,' he says; 'I'm confident that whoever comes in here will love me. How could anyone not?'

'Trust,' I would say, like so many other dog owners, as I mercilessly placed a tempting mini-morsel six inches from the dog's nose, tormenting the poor animal simply in order to prove which of us was really in charge. 'Trust,' I would repeat, in a voice just a little more on edge, as Mitzpah surreptitiously slid his mouth an inch closer. 'Trust,' I would find myself repeating more anxiously as his look became even more intent; followed by a hasty, 'Eat!' hopefully at least a moment before it became too late, releasing both him and me from the growing suspense, and proving that my trust was only slightly greater than the minuscule piece of food which Mitzpah now gobbled up while giving me a sidelong look as if to say, 'Was all that really worth it just for this?'

There's no such thing as a relationship without trust, including those with dogs. But, as in many human connections, the trust on either side is often very unequal.

We have to trust our animals to know the basic rules of behaviour. If there were such a thing as a Ten Commandments for Dogs, it would no doubt include such basics as, 'Don't bite, don't steal, and don't relieve yourself indoors.' But, unlike with adults, where each person is answerable for his or her own actions, what our dogs do remains our responsibility.

I laughed when a friend told me his dog had eaten another family's picnic: 'He was running so far ahead that I couldn't catch him up. By the time I got there, it was too late. I apologised and offered to pay, but there was nothing I could do to put it right. It was so embarrassing.' I found it less amusing when Mitzpah was – almost – the culprit. We were out late on a walk, when the dog and I simultaneously spotted a gathering of young people holding a midnight celebration. They were seated in a circle at the centre of which I saw, to my horror, a large, sumptuous candlelit birthday cake. The dog was in front of me, but I doubled my pace, shouted out, caught the group's attention, and managed to arrive breathless but neck-to-neck with the eager animal. Mercifully the revellers had detected the threat and were laughing cheerfully as they held the cake aloft. Mitzpah, to his credit, ran on with seeming nonchalance. When, a few weeks later during an innocent walk in the New Forest, he came across a plate of sandwiches unwisely placed on the ground at the intersection between two paths as if in a deliberate appeal for canine company, I couldn't really blame him for helping himself to a cheese slice. Sometimes it isn't the dog's fault.

There are certain additional rules which dogs have to obey in Jewish households. In this regard, there's the unusual case of the dog who ate the mezuzah, the thin roll of parchment containing the injunction 'to love the Lord your God', which is traditionally fixed to the doorpost of every Jewish home. Normally, the small scroll is placed in a case, often of silver or carved wood, before being pinned into position. But in this instance our friends had only recently moved into their new flat and had just found time to attach the mezuzah, uncovered and unprotected, with a lump of Blu-Tack. The next day it had vanished. Suspicion fell on their long-legged and ever-hungry hound for reaching up and eating the leather scroll. The words on it were, however, holy; pious Jews often touch their hand against the mezuzah and kiss their fingers out of respect when entering or leaving a house. What was to be done in this unusual instance? According to one rabbinical opinion, the only solution was to kiss the dog instead, since he had become the unintentional vessel for the sacred text.

There are, however, more serious offences. I have to blame myself, and my dogs, for the occasional breaches of the code of trust according to which society, dog owners and dogs interrelate. Safi used to feel that he was responsible for me whenever we left the house. Unfortunately, this would sometimes mean that he took a dim of view of other dogs who came too close, especially Alsatians. From time to time he would set about chasing them off with fearless, and annoying, determination. I had to keep a very sharp eye. Jewish law teaches that we must acknowledge our sins to ourselves, tell them truthfully to God, apologise, make good to anyone who has suffered on our account, and ensure that we don't commit the same transgressions again. But we don't have to proclaim our own, let alone anyone else's, faults to the public at large. I am working on the assumption that this holds good for dogs as well. It is not therefore fitting for me to disclose to the public at large any further details of canine misdemeanours.

Far deeper than the trust a human has to place in his or her dog is the trust a dog has to place in his or her human. We have the power to control virtually every facet of our dog's life: when she eats and gets her walks; whether she's kept clean and in good health or left dirty and unkempt; whether she is treated with affection or subject to violence. We even determine the amount of space she has to roam in, from open country down to a cage in which the animal can scarcely turn around or escape its own filth. The opportunities for cruelty are as endless as those for love.

Safi came to us with his trust profoundly injured, but not broken. From that first moment when he licked our faces, he was a canine exemplar of the triumph of hope over experience. Perhaps this was because, although he was betrayed by whoever pushed him out of the car in an unknown part of town, his initial impressions of life were of firm and loving care. I hope we managed to give him back his confidence after the trauma of his abandonment. For his part, he never until his dying day took us for granted. It wasn't just that he hated to leave our side, or even to let us out of his sight for more than the shortest of intervals. He had a gentle presence. 'He's such a kind dog,' my parents said, soon after they had met him for the first time. Fourteen years later, when he died, they said the same. There was something about his manner which conveyed a sense of gratitude, as if he were regularly telling us in the non-verbal language of dogs: 'Thank you for giving me back a life with so much love. Thank you for restoring my confidence.'

When trust is honoured, it grows imperceptibly into faithfulness. I read somewhere that it's a pity the authors of the Bible, and Shakespeare too, had a negative view of dogs as fierce and fickle. Couldn't they also have seen in them exemplars of loving faithfulness? The Hebrew word for faith, *emunah*, does not refer to a series of dogmas, a set of principles by which the believer is distinguished from the atheist. Rather, it means trust, what the prophet Micah described as 'walking humbly with God' by living according to the values which tradition and our own intuitions teach us that God wants of us. Foremost among these is *chesed*, faithful kindness towards all living beings, a love which indicates a close and respectful bond with life itself and every living thing. Thus, *emunah* means loving, trusting loyalty. In this regard, our dogs are not just our followers, but often our teachers too.

In essence, trust is mutual, a heartfelt partnership. A bold Jewish teaching puts the following words into God's mouth: 'Your candle is in my hands; and my candle is in your hands.' The first part of the sentence is unsurprising; we know that we do not and cannot control our ultimate destiny. But in what way is God's candle in our hands? What authority or power do we have over God? I believe the words refer to the power and influence bestowed on us over so much which is precious to the God of life: our own existence and the quality of life of those close to us, including the people, animals and even plants we affect through our conduct, because all living being is interconnected and we all belong to the same sacred oneness.

Dogs express this in simpler, less pious terms. Mitzpah rolls over onto his back and waves his paws in the air as our guests enter our home. I trust life, he says; I'm confident that whoever comes in here will love me. How could anyone not?

Dogs not only demonstrate trust and love but also awaken it in others. 'The puppy feels the opposite of a gun,' wrote Caitlin Moran in a recent column in *The Times Magazine*, describing the effect on everyone they met of her recently acquired nine-week-old pet, Luna. 'By holding it in my hands and pointing it at people, I can make them come alive.'

However much self-protection, cynicism or anxiety may lead us to armour our heart, it would be tragic if we lost forever that simple faith in life which puppies and dogs so often show, despite everything we've done to their species.

14
Kinship

*If they're different from us,
we're liable to be suspicious*

Jewish tradition is at once reverent, imaginative and subversive in its attitude to its sacred texts. This applies no less to that most frequently quoted verse of all than it does to the rest of the Bible: 'Love your neighbour as yourself.' There are plain readings, mystical readings and creative misreadings, all of which have insights to yield, even for the relationship between a human and his or her dog.

The first question has to be whether or not a dog can

qualify as 'your neighbour'? Here, the original Hebrew may prove helpful. The word so widely translated as 'neighbour' is *re'a*, which in fact means 'companion' or 'friend'. If 'a dog is a man's best friend', then surely my dog is also my neighbour and I must love him, or her, as myself. After all, we may well spend more time in the company of our dog than of any other living being. The dog sits by our feet when we read, sets off with us on our daily walks, travels with us in the car, and sleeps under, by the foot of, or even, if spoilt, on the bed. For many people, a dog is their closest companion.

My guess is that most dog lovers experience little difficulty in loving their pets as well as themselves. It's not our dogs which are the issue; it's our human neighbours who constitute the problem. As the lyricist Alan Jay Lerner has Doolittle sing in *My Fair Lady*, God may have wanted us to help our neighbours, but what's to prevent us from kocking on their door precisely when we're sure they're not at home? Who's to know that we haven't tried our best? The world would be a much better place if only we cared for all the human beings in our neighbourhoods as well as many of us do for our dogs, whether those people are like ourselves in faith, ethnicity, style or tastes, or not. The love of animals is no excuse for prejudice, unkindness or indifference towards the human beings around us who need our friendship, solidarity and compassion just as much, and probably even more.

There's a deeply uncomfortable reading, or rather

misreading, of the famous words from the Bible. Rather than loving our neighbour as we love ourselves, we love our neighbours 'like ourselves', that is, so long as they are like us in religion, colour, nationality or even income. If they're different from us, we're liable to be suspicious, nervous, ignorant or downright aggressive.

Even dogs have been co-opted into this misconstruction of the biblical message. Literature contains many examples of how bigoted owners use dogs to protect their privileges by keeping unwanted neighbours at bay, just because they are different or poor. 'Thou hast seen a farmer's dog bark at a beggar?' Shakespeare's King Lear asks the blinded and bewildered Earl of Gloucester. 'And the creature run from the cur? There thou mightst behold the great image of authority: a dog's obeyed in office.'

Dogs have been used throughout history to drive away the outsider, the indigent, the neighbour who isn't like oneself. Jewish tradition long ago castigated those who allow their dogs to frighten poor or needy people away from their door. Jews, who rarely kept dogs as pets until the twentieth century, often found themselves confronted by the threatening growls and bared teeth of the animals of those who held them in contempt.

Nazi guards frequently trained dogs to savage their victims. The Alsatians in the concentration camps were not vicious because of the intrinsic nature of their breed, but because their handlers taught them to embody their own hatreds. The dogs of some of the most notorious Nazis were all too familiar to their prisoners. They knew them by name, and feared them. Amon Göth, commandant of the Płaszów concentration camp outside Krakow (where, at its fullest in 1944, twenty-five thousand prisoners were held in abject misery) personally murdered many inmates, assisted by his two dogs Rolf and Ralf, who tore them to death. Victims of racism, trafficking and hatred across the world have learnt to fear the dogs of their so-called masters.

Nicky was walking through a nearby park with Mitzpah when a man on a bench called out to her to take care and keep him on the lead. Noticing her puzzlement, he explained: 'Yesterday a woman just like you came by with her poodle. A man with a large dog was sitting on this same bench I'm on now. He let his dog attack the woman's pet. She begged him to call the animal off but he just laughed. It killed the poodle in the end.'

This incident may provide insight into a question almost invariably raised in any discussion about loving one's neighbour as oneself: what if you don't love yourself? Perhaps such people feel no love within themselves, and their dogs become the embodiment of their own aggression. Perhaps they even see themselves as the victim; the violence of the dog expresses their unconscious feeling of being under constant attack from their own thoughts.

The mystics had yet another different, and more daring, interpretation of loving your neighbour. Focusing on the end of the verse, 'as yourself, I am the Lord', the eighteenth-century rabbi known as the Baal Shem Tov, the Master of the Good Name, explained that just as we behave towards our neighbour, so God behaves towards us. God shadows our conduct. If we treat others kindly, God is close and kind to us; if we behave hard-heartedly, God is harsh and remote from us. He wanted to stress the hypocrisy and futility of wanting God to help us if we refuse to help others. We cannot ask God, or other people, to be merciful to us if we ourselves show no mercy.

Perhaps, in a similar way, our dogs mirror us too. They say that dogs look like their owners, which I've always taken as an undeserved compliment since, unlike me, Mitzpah is both good-looking and photogenic. Dogs often also behave like their owners. 'A dog is morally neutral,' a friend who's a vet once told me, meaning that canine characteristics are largely acquired, rather than inborn. Our dogs, it would then follow, are often a reflection of who we are: hostile or friendly, gentle or aggressive. Or perhaps we choose dogs that express the kind of person we want to be, or fantasise that we actually are. Unless, as so often happens, it's our dogs who've chosen us.

Of course, this isn't the whole truth; dogs have their qualities too. Some are almost untameably shy, or assertive. Some are wonderful with people, but difficult with their fellow quadrupeds. Some may be vicious by nature. Others have had bad experiences long before they join our family and no amount of love can cure their fear, or aggression. The best we can manage in such cases is to take them for canine behaviour modification therapy.

By contrast, there are also dogs who maintain a loving and gentle nature despite exposure to the utmost cruelty, and who, with long-suffering patience that is painful to behold, lick the hand that beats them.

Yet dogs often really are rather like us and our households. The dog who greets everyone with an eager, tail-wagging welcome, who rolls over to have its tummy rubbed, the dog with an affectionate gaze and licking tongue, probably expresses a kindness and openness to others which characterise its human family too. No doubt I'm just a sentimental romantic for believing that most dogs come to the same conclusion as the Reverend Martin Luther King when he declared: 'I have decided to stick with love. Hate is too great a burden to bear.'

15
Acceptance

When he could no longer manage the steps, he would wait
at the top of the landing for me to carry him down

Safi was almost fifteen when Mitzpah joined our
family. Taking them for a walk together was an experience best avoided. Mitzpah would be out in front,
pulling on his lead, while Safi would advance at a painful
geriatric limp. I would find myself stretched out in the
middle, arms akimbo, trying to keep Mitzpah in check
without tugging at poor Safi's neck.

I used to wonder how Safi felt: did he remember when
he used to be the dog trotting merrily in front, setting

the pace for his humans? Did he miss his frisky, three-walks-a-day youth? Or was I projecting onto him my own regret at the passing of his life, while he remained content, more or less, in the immediate present of his now?

Dogs, my wife tells me, and many of my dog-loving friends agree, aren't like that: they don't chew over the past, suffer remorse or harbour recriminations, and they don't worry about the future. They live in the present; they accept their circumstances and their fate.

They're accepting of others too, most of the time, as long as their homes aren't invaded and so long as no new-fangled arrival alienates the affection of their owners. There doesn't appear to be such a thing as dog racism. My Welsh Border Collie is made to feel perfectly welcome in Scotland, Germany or France. One doesn't see poodles only greeting other poodles in the street, or spaniels only sniffing spaniels. A Labrador will lower its nose to the tail of a corgi, and a dachshund jump up at a Dalmatian. They may chase cats, but that's a different matter; among other dogs they don't discriminate on grounds of colour, breeding, race or social class. There's no such a thing as a park for some kinds of dog only.

They're also accepting of their own stage and status in life, so long – and it's a big so long – as they have a decent home and aren't made subject to cruelty.

Safi grew old graciously. When he could no longer

manage the steps, he would wait at the top landing for me to carry him down. Most nights he would need to pay at least one visit to the garden. I would lift him up, take him downstairs and carefully set him back on his feet, anxious not to jolt his aching hips. He would go outside to do what was necessary before waiting once more for me to lift him back upstairs to our bedroom, where he slept underneath our bed.

I never saw him fret at the top of the staircase. He waited, patiently. He didn't try to manage on his own, or show irritation at the lack of his former agility. He knew he couldn't manage and he trusted me to help him. He didn't chafe at the limitations of his present state, incapacitating as they were. 'Don't kick against the pricks' advises the Bible in Acts 9:5, and Safi never did. It's a challenge many of us humans find considerably less easy, though I understand that some dogs also become morose when they lose the ability to run, roll and rejoice in the sunlight, like they used to do.

Nowadays there are mobility aids for dogs too. As one website says: 'If you care for an older, injured, or disabled pet, you have come to the right place! A wheelchair, accessories or other aid will make them mobile again, ready to play and get exercise for a more happy and healthy life.' Another site advertises itself as 'presenting your dog's new best friend': wheelchairs which are 'lightweight, portable, comfortable, length and width adjustable, suitable for inside and outdoors'.

'Wheelchair' doesn't seem quite the right description, since the dog doesn't sit in the apparatus, which supports the stomach, hips and back legs. It's more like a canine Zimmer frame, except for the rear end to rest on rather than the front.

These aids give dogs, like people, a new lease of mobility.

I can't imagine dogs take to such equipment without balking at their strangeness, at least initially. But I doubt if pride, stubbornness, the refusal to acknowledge their disability or embarrassment at their declined state keep them from giving it a try. I've seen dogs with such 'wheelchairs' walking, for all I could tell, quite happily across the park.

Dogs seem to accept their own ageing and dying too. A colleague whose dog had not long ago passed away told me how all the family had wept over her while she lay sick in her basket. 'Do you think she knew?' I asked him. 'No,' he replied. 'We were crying; our tears fell on her face. What troubled her was why we were so sad, not the fact that she was going to die, if she was aware of it at all.'

I remain uncertain. One hears of cats, and sometimes dogs, going off into a secret, private space to die alone. Perhaps they need the quiet; perhaps they don't want anyone to see; perhaps they prefer to be on their own in these final moments of transition with whatever they intuit as the presence of God. People, too, often die alone. They depart from this world in those few minutes when, after hours of sitting by the bedside, the family go off to have a much-needed cup of tea or take a gulp of fresh air. Later, their relatives are full of self-blame: 'Why did I have to go out just when . . .' But maybe there are certain experiences which cannot be shared and which the spirit understands that it has to experience alone. The parting of the dying from the living often occurs, slowly and half imperceptibly, before the final severance of death.

Maybe it's easier for dogs to be accepting. It appears, though we can never know for sure, that they form no expectations of the future and aren't beset other than momentarily by disappointment when events turn out differently from what we imagine the dog might have hoped. But that doesn't seem to me to account for the entire difference between us and them. There's something else as well, a kind of humility which animals convey: they move in harmony with life, they don't assert themselves in pride against our mortal destiny. They don't take Dylan Thomas's advice and 'rage against the dying of the light'.

The rabbis of the second century puzzled over the commandment, repeated in the Jewish daily liturgy morning, evening and night: 'You shall love the Lord your God with all your heart, with all your life and with all your might'. They were clear about how they understood heart and life, but how were we to love God with all our might? The Hebrew term *me'odecha* is obscure; what was loving God with it supposed to mean? Playing on the word alliteratively, they chose to explain it in terms which amount to the greatest challenge any of us ultimately has to face: 'Whatever measure of fortune God metes out to you, acknowledge God most constantly and deeply.' In other words, though of course we want to do our utmost to make our lot in life and the lot of others better, in the end we have to try not only to accept our fate, but to do so with thankfulness and humility. The alternative is bitterness and resentment.

Dogs, it seems, may be better at this modest art than we are.

In the wild Scottish Highlands

He curves back round from the moors to check on me, before racing off once more

The guidebook describes it as 'a long slog'. But it's a walk I love, and fear. It begins just east of Loch Maree, famous for its many small islands and the rare black-throated divers which breed by its waters. The loch runs for twelve miles east to west before a short river connects it with Loch Ewe, which opens onto the sea. Here the convoys gathered in the Second World War before embarking on the dangerous voyage to Murmansk with supplies of armour for the Russians, or crossing the treacherous North Atlantic, rife with its hidden packs of U-boats. The twenty-two-mile walk climbs and twists above the northern shoreline of the loch as far as the isolated estate of Letterewe, where it turns to zigzag up a steep mountain pass before descending into a parallel glen and heading across bare moorlands, past bleak lochans and finally through a pine forest towards the welcome cafés of Poolewe.

Mitzpah and I take the small highland road from Kinlochewe to the tiny village of Incheril. I look up at the sky; the forecast is fair, but the scattered clouds could easily gather into a blanket of impenetrable grey, bringing driving rain. The route is sufficiently remote that a mistake in reading the map or a sudden change in the weather could have challenging consequences. A tinge of fear disturbs me as I set out once again on this remote and rarely chosen path. Some inner need summons me to another encounter with loneliness and awe. On similar walks, there are signs to warn the unprepared: 'You are now entering uninhabited territory; ensure that you are adequately provisioned and have appropriate equipment.' Mitzpah invariably pays scant attention to such notices and heads off into the heather undeterred.

At least this time I have him for company. Once, when the driver of the local bus said 'no dogs' in a tone which brooked no pleading, I trekked the long, deserted way entirely on my own, something I would never have chosen to do. On another occasion, my daughter Libbi came with me, a great walking companion, but the numerous flies and midges which preferred her to me made much of her day a misery. I've also walked in nearby hills with Mossy, an equally enthusiastic hiker, on one occasion fording several streams in spate with a reluctant Mitzpah swimming behind in tow on his lead. But, on this particular route, it's usually just me and the dog.

As we reach the gate where the path swerves away from the village, I see a small laminated paper pinned to the wooden crossbar: 'To James, who ascended Slioch, but only the mists came down.' I look up towards the stony bulk of the mountain, hunched in stolid dominance over the northern shore of Loch Maree, its rocky base rising in many places in sharp-edged cliffs straight out of the water. Unease, previously as thin as the high cloud, descends inside me, with a penetrating sense of my smallness, the irrelevance of my life and death. My own route doesn't involve climbing Slioch, only crossing for several miles the outcrops above its feet, above the crags which fall steeply into the depths of the loch.

I re-read the notice and wonder who James was, and what he meant to the person who placed this eloquent, understated note. It reminds me of the plaque with the names of all the dead, fixed to a rock above the nearby Fairy Lochs by Shieldaig, where a B-24 Liberator bomber crashed on its way home after the war. It was taking American servicemen back across the North Atlantic to the safety of their families when it lost height in thick fog and struck the hills. The remnants of the aeroplane, small pieces of steel, parts of an engine, the rubber from a tattered tyre, the wing of a propeller protruding above the placid water, still lie scattered across the rocks and lochans all around. The quiet beauty of the place makes a strange contrast with the violence of the impact that scattered this wreckage and killed all the crew and passengers. Their spirit is now embraced in the silence of the hills, the wind, and the drift of lily leaves on the placid surface of the water.

I turn to follow the signpost: Poolewe by way of Letterewe. I put the dog back on the lead as we traverse the damp fields until we've passed the last of the grazing sheep. Then I let him free onto the hills.

After an hour, we reach the shallow tailwaters of the loch and, crossing the bridge over a waterfall, climb past the parting where the better-used path turns north into a different glen. Then we trek, mile upon mile, along the faint remnants of the way which long ago the postman would traverse twice or more each week, ten miles in each direction, carrying parcels to the lonely Letterewe estate. One of the managers told me that once or twice each year they still drive the horses out that way, to take them to fresh grazing. We pass through swathes of shoulder-high bracken, beneath which the path is entirely invisible for hundreds of yards at a time. I'm forced to trust my feet to sense the slightly flatter, harder earth which may, or may not, indicate that here was once a well-trodden route, long hidden beneath the lush growth.

Mitzpah shows no such uncertainty. He smells his way merrily forward and runs ahead with canine sure-footedness, while I try to keep my eye on the movement of the ferns, the only indication of his presence as he disturbs the bottom of their stems. But, sensing that for once it's I who am depending on him, he turns and pauses every couple of minutes to check if I'm still following. At least on this part of the route it's easy to keep our bearings, walking as best we can along an uneven parallel between the loch below and the ridge of the mountain above. Eventually we descend to a solid bridge over a river and reach the secluded estate with its baronial house, chapel and carefully tended fields, without encountering a single soul. Nevertheless, I feel relief to have arrived amid habitation in this region sometimes known as Britain's final wilderness, where the previous owner wanted to reintroduce wolves, had his early death not prevented him. An arrow advises walkers to keep outside the periphery of the grounds.

Above us is the pass which leads to Dubh Loch, the 'black loch', Fionn Loch and, eventually, the sea. I check my map and compass and, still uncertain, test out several possible paths. The first comes to a sudden end, forcing me back down a muddy descent. The next climbs so steeply for a thousand feet that I'm obliged to pause repeatedly to regain my breath and strength. It's not until we cross between the crags at the summit and I see the sand-coloured track winding westwards far below that I feel some abatement of my fear. Only now do I feel confident that I'm not lost. I pray this path will not end, like its partner, in the middle of nowhere, that it won't desert me in this semi-wasteland where, for several further hours, I meet no traveller, only stones and water, grey-green grass, bog myrtle and reeds. From time to time, small brown birds cry out in startled warning as they rise in front of my feet. 'Mitzpah,' I call periodically, 'Mitzpah'; and he curves back round from the moors below to check on me, before racing off once more.

It's mid-afternoon when the clouds unite to exclude the last blue patches of sky. A thin drizzle develops into slanting grey rain. The narrow path ascends and drops, climbs and falls, till I wonder if it is taking me in any direction at all. But at length the dim green edge of the Kernsary Forest cuts across the hills. Entering it, I slip repeatedly on the muddy, rain-puddled track which passes steeply between the dense conifers. Emerging into the milder moorland below, I finally see another living creature, a sheep, the first land animal for many miles, and call out instinctively in greeting, mammal to mammal. Though the creature doesn't so much as deign to lift its head, I'm nonetheless glad of this encounter and feel an immediate warmth of companionship. Mercifully, Mitzpah doesn't notice.

Footsore, I arrive with Mitzpah at the field of horses,

which graze peacefully in the meadows of the Kernsary estate. What joy, as the re-emerging sun illumines the apple-green grass. But the intermission is brief; the final miles of the walk are a weary plod through increasingly heavy rain. Mitzpah prances ahead undaunted; he was born to run among the steep hills of South Wales: why should the mere fact that this happens to be the Highlands of Scotland deter his native enthusiasm? The rain seems not to bother him, the loneliness not to touch him, so long as he knows I'm near. And I, too, like to know that he's not far from my side.

Five times I've completed that walk, drawn to its lonely challenges between the rocks and the water, the empty moorland and the louring sky. I ask myself what compels me to return to these bleak though beautiful places. The question takes me once again by instinctive association to that elemental moment in Shakespeare's *King Lear* when the blind Earl of Gloucester recognises the deranged monarch wandering in helpless madness on the tops of the cliffs near Dover. Moved by intuitive fealty, he wants to kiss his master's hand: 'Let me wipe it first,' the humbled Lear replies. 'It smells of mortality.' Amid these bare mountains, I breathe in the smell of my own mortality.

The Bible speaks of the fear, as well as the love, of God. The medieval Jewish philosopher Maimonides describes this as a moment of retreat. Love is a movement forward in wonder; fear is the corresponding step back, overwhelmed by the sense of one's own ignorance and frailty before the vast, enduring majesty of creation. Perhaps awe would be a better translation than fear; the awe which silences the spirit in the awareness of the ceaseless cycle of creation and destruction, in which the heart is made, refined, attuned, undone, dissolved, annihilated and re-absorbed into this ever-encompassing entirety in which it is nothing except one tiny apprehending particle in the infinite consciousness of God.

I set out year after year on that long and lonely walk because I want to be humbled, to be put back in my place within creation. Amid these rocks and waters my body could rot down in what would scarcely constitute a single second in their slow narrative of aeons, my bones disintegrating into the meagre layer of earth in which only the thin grass of the moorland is able to flourish. I have an inner need to encounter my suscep-tibility to death, not by reading about war, terror and accidents, or witnessing illness and the slow decline of age, but here, in this setting of elemental space, fash-ioned over ages amid which human lifespans shrink to nothing; here where I might be, like Wordsworth's beloved and lamented Lucy, 'Rolled round in earth's diurnal course/With rocks and stones and trees.'

And precisely here I need my dog for company. We affirm together the solidarity of mortal existence before the vast inanimate mass of boulder and gully, overhang and col. We both draw breath, we both need food, we both feel fear, we both rejoice in the sheer delight of sun and cooling water. This is our dance together, my dog's and mine. I am not sure whether Mitzpah intuits anything of such matters; perhaps, on the contrary, it's the fact that he is able to delight undaunted in this disturbing landscape which brings me joy and solace. Maybe that's why I engage in this encounter with so much more confidence when he is by my side.

Yet I also experience a deep sense of belonging amid these hills and streams, in the scent of the mountain air, where the small birds fly up out of the wild grass, and the red-black glow of the long, western twilight and the curlew's dusk cry across the darkening water hold my soul enamoured amid their haunting beauty.

The track broadens into a tarmacked path and at last becomes a proper road as we near the bridge over the short river which carries the headwaters of Loch Maree through to Loch Ewe and out to the Atlantic Ocean. I fail to comprehend the patience of the fishermen, standing stoically next to their rods at their mid-river posts in the rapid rush of water, despite the wind and rain. I know, too, from being trapped at the end of long walks on the wrong side of such speeding currents, how readily the swirling, glittering waves and eddies can mesmerise the brain and confuse the dizzy mind in the critical challenge of maintaining one's balance against the power of the coursing water.

Cold and soaked, Mitzpah collapses happily on the

carpeted floor of a bar in Poolewe, where I order a tea for myself and request a bowl of water for him together with some biscuits, which, of course, we share. A few minutes later, Nicky and the children join us; I'm delighted to be back with my family, in the company of people.

That night, I watch Mitzpah dream, his front paws moving with increasing rapidity as if he were chasing the water down a cascading burn or racing up the steepening incline to where the ridge of the mountain encounters the sky.

Weeks later, when the Torah refers to our relationship with animals, I mention in a sermon that I spoke to a sheep out of a feeling of kinship among the rocks and water, adding that the animal was too busy grazing to say anything in reply. Afterwards a gentleman new to the congregation turned to the person next to him and asked in a loud whisper: 'Is your rabbi always mad?' I learnt about this interchange only because that person happened to be my son.

16
Mortality

Some dogs yield to loving care; others hide, and try to lick their wounds, alone

If the 'w' word had to be avoided because of the immediate response of excessive enthusiasm, the 'v' word was ruled out because of the fear it instantly evoked. Both our dogs had an uncanny understanding of when they were being taken to the vet.

Mitzpah often refuses to get out of the car, requiring us to lift him ignominiously off the back seat and deposit him on the pavement, where he makes determined efforts to head off in the opposite direction from the surgery.

There have even been times when we've parked in all innocence, without even realising the vet's was nearby, and only understood his insistence on remaining in the vehicle when we passed the dreaded frontage ten doors down the street. This is puzzling, because in general Mitzpah is less prone to fear than Safi, who used to turn into a pathetic, heart-rending, dribbling jelly during thunderstorms and whenever there were fireworks. He would try to hide by putting his head under the bed or inside a cupboard, but nothing could ever entirely calm his fear. In contrast, Mitzpah, who barks at aeroplanes and underground trains as if to say, 'I'm bigger than you', simply seeks our presence when thunder threatens and lies anxiously nearby. It seems to make little difference how friendly the receptionists, nurses and vets actually are, and they're almost invariably extremely kind. Mitzpah either crouches underneath the chairs in the waiting room or tries to climb onto my or Nicky's lap. I remember one occasion in France, where he needed his statutory injections before returning to the UK, when I had to pick him up from under a bench and carry him into the surgery like an upset toddler while trying to avoid knocking large numbers of packets of worming tablets and dog shampoo off the shelves with his dangling tail.

Mitzpah finds the procedures once inside the surgery no less humiliating. He invariably resists standing on the table, for which I can scarcely blame him. He generally cringes in the corner by the door, where, paying especial attention to his sharp teeth, I have to hold him tightly to enable the vet to examine him. His worst moment came when preparing once again for a return trip home to London. We were in Amsterdam, towards the end of our long walk north up the Rhine, and had made an appointment at a high street surgery. The next day we were due to take the ferry back to Harwich and he therefore needed his injections that evening. The film crew had asked permission to record the consultation. The vet insisted on taking Mitzpah's temperature, doing so by means of the time-honoured method of sticking the thermometer up his backside. The entire scene was filmed, to the dog's evident dismay. I could feel him thinking: 'They'd never allow a human to be humiliated like that.'

In one respect, though, I have to admire both Safi's and Mitzpah's conduct. On several occasions, I watched them both have blood taken without so much as flinching for a millisecond. This was a considerable improvement over the reactions of their owner, who more than once, when a child, found himself coming round from a faint on the surgery floor after a similar procedure. Watching the dogs, I vowed to emulate them and keep entirely calm in future, a resolution which I've managed, more or less, to keep.

Mitzpah is always delighted when the moment comes to leave the surgery. He generally gives vent to his relief before we're even fully outside by lifting his leg against the doorpost, though mercifully always on the external side, and releasing a stream of contemptuous disapproval.

But the trouble is not always over when we go back home. Often we're carrying with us a small packet of tablets which we have to get down the reluctant animal's throat: 'Two every day with his meal and one of the larger tablets last thing at night.' Safi was definitely the worse culprit for surreptitiously spitting his medicine back out. It didn't seem to matter how well we thought we'd managed to conceal the pill in cheese, tuna, or even his favourite challah. He was rarely deceived. No less simple was applying ointment to the dogs' assorted sores. During our long walks around London and through Germany, I was worried that Mitzpah's pads would suffer. But my efforts to protect them were to little avail; I would no sooner reach for the pot of protective cream than he would dive under the bed, where I would gingerly reach in to tackle one paw at a time. Three seconds later I would observe him licking the application off, while periodically squinting at me with a look of vindicated pride.

However, it was different when either dog was really in pain. Safi was out walking with my mother when a squirrel he was chasing had the wit to turn on him and bite. The dog came crying back and waited patiently for her to attend to the small, but deep and painful, wound. If Mitzpah gets a thorn in his paw, he stops and waits for me to extract it. Sometimes, if I make a sudden or injudicious move, he threatens to growl or snap. But then he restrains himself and licks my hand in apology, knowing that what I'm doing is really for his good. 'Sorry,' he seems to say, 'I'm rather scared, but I appreciate that you're trying to help.'

Like every other dog, Safi and Mitzpah hated wearing those ghastly lampshades round their necks to prevent them from biting or scratching at an open wound. They found it impossible to adjust to their new width and would frequently bump into the doorposts and furniture. They would also bash into us, teaching us to give them a wide berth. Once, in sheer affection, Safi jumped up at me, cutting open the bridge of my nose. But it wasn't just the physical nuisance; the shades were also a source of embarrassment. On one occasion, Nicky and I were all but certain that the reason Safi had tugged fiercely on his lead was to force us to cross the road, in order to avoid being seen by a neighbourhood dog while encumbered with this unsightly collar.

I've sometimes wondered whether the dogs feared the vet's because they somehow intuited that this was where their days might one day cease. I can't answer for them, but I speak for myself when I say that a low chord of pain reverberates in me whenever I have to take Mitzpah to the same surgery where Safi's life, albeit mercifully, was ended.

It's not only dogs who feel an instinctive fear when they have to go for their annual check-up. As humans, we learn to treat an ordinary visit to the doctor as something of a routine. But I doubt if we ever entirely dismiss from the back of our mind the possibility that the results of the blood test will not turn out quite as they ought. 'I think I should send you for a further examination; I'm sure it's really nothing, but just in case.' We thank the doctor and say, 'Of course', but already our thoughts are deep into the landscape of 'what if?' We know that we're mortal, but, at the same time, we also don't *know*. It's not just, as my father used to say, that we haven't been told the date on the return half of the ticket which brought us into this world; it's that the impersonal truth that we're all vulnerable and all one day going to die feels utterly different when it becomes an immediate personal reality: 'The less good news is that I'm afraid it is a form of cancer. The better news is that it's eminently curable, especially as we've caught it early. Still, I think you should go for . . .' We try to take in the subsequent instructions about appointments, tests and further diagnoses, but the ground beneath us has begun to spin and the doctor's words appear like the writing on the wall we see in flashes each dizzying rotation. We are too shocked by the overall meaning to comprehend the details.

I'm often asked whether there are special prayers for a sick pet, or what to do when a beloved animal dies.

From time to time I receive an email: 'Are there Jewish prayers for when your dog is ill?' I don't write a reply but pick up the phone. 'We're desperately worried; she's been with us for thirteen years. She's such a wonderful dog. The children have grown up with her. She goes everywhere with us. We won't know what to do with ourselves if anything should happen.'

When I reach the special daily blessing in which we ask God for healing, I mention the name of the sick dog alongside the names of all those whose relatives have asked me to include them in my prayers. I don't consider it an insult to the unique value of human life to ask for God to care for animals too. After all, the Psalmist taught that 'God's mercies are upon all God's works' (Psalm 145). I don't necessarily believe in a God who will intervene from heaven, set aside the laws of nature and bring this particular animal back to perfect health at the cost of an alternative miracle the deity might have performed instead. Rather, I want to open my heart to the sacred bond of vitality and compassion in which all being is encompassed, hoping that life will bring healing to all for whom we care, and that through this prayer I may become a source of help and comfort too. We cannot prevent death, or stop irreversible illness, but we can hold each other in the loving embrace of life.

A couple of days later I receive a call, 'Thank God, the dog's much better. We don't know what we would have done . . .' When I ask further, I learn that the dog is back home and the family are on shifts by day and night so as not to leave her alone in her pain. 'There's still anxiety in her looks. And she needs her medicine. And her bandage has to be changed every twenty-four hours. But it's amazing, and sad, the trust in her eyes when we have to touch her near where she had her stitches.' Perhaps dogs are rather like us: some yield to loving care with appreciative submission; others hide, and try to lick their wounds alone.

Sadly I know that on another occasion the words I hear will be different: 'The children are inconsolable and I'm finding it impossible to know what to say to them because I'm so broken inside myself.'

I look at Mitzpah and say to myself, even as I know it to be a vain thought: 'May he be healthy for ever.'

17
Grieving

I'd been watching with a growing sense of anguish how his step was becoming less even, his limp more pronounced

During all the nights when Safi was old and needed to be carried down the stairs, I never resented the four-in-the-morning interruption to our sleep. He trusted me tenderly and I, in turn, owed him this faithfulness. Besides, love does not keep a tally of favours. I just wanted him to live.

When, in addition, he grew deaf, I would have to go and look for him among the dark shadows of the predawn garden and guide him indoors, before carrying him back up the stairs.

Then came the shocking evening when, in front of startled guests, he spread out his back legs and urinated copiously on the carpet. That was when it became impossible to doubt any longer that the canine equivalent of dementia had overcome him. For several months a bucket and rags were frequently on call, together with carpet cleaner and dog smell remover. We never told Safi off, and indeed our guests that night fell instantly quiet the moment we explained. Everyone knew only too well what dementia can mean. Over time we observed, with growing dread, how standing had become difficult for him; how, when endeavouring to lie himself down, he shifted each leg slowly, inch by inch, how every movement clearly brought him suffering. Eventually we were forced to acknowledge that there was no posture he could adopt in which he didn't feel pain. The days had come in which it was impossible for us to pretend to ourselves that he wasn't hurting, virtually all the time.

'It's the love which keeps him going,' a friend had observed some months earlier as she watched the dog make his slow way down the steps, placing each paw with trepidation, before the challenge had simply become too great for him to manage, or for us to bear watching. But there comes a point where the love becomes selfish. It didn't feel right to make the dog suffer because of our inability to bear the parting.

A year earlier he had been diagnosed with cancer. Concerned that he had developed a persistent cough, we had taken Safi to our vet, who had discovered a round, ball-like growth in his side. He recommended surgery at The Queen Mother Animal Hospital in South Mimms. It fell to me to take him to the initial appointment. Within an hour, he had been examined, X-rayed and we'd been offered a diagnosis. I remember feeling torn between appreciation for this alacritous care and the thought that it was utterly absurd for such a facility to be available for animals, admittedly at a price, while humans had to wait weeks at best for a similar service, while many never had access to anything remotely comparable at any point in their entire lives.

'The treatment should give him another year, if something else doesn't get him first,' we were advised. Safi was already at least fourteen. We chose to proceed with the operation. After handing him over to the staff, I remember going outside, holding on to the fence by the neighbouring field and weeping. 'Buckets,' said Nicky, admitting she'd done the same. Not long after Safi came round from the anaesthetic, we received a phone call from one of the veterinary nurses: 'He's such a humanised dog and so hates being in a pen that we've allowed him to follow us around the ICU with his drip attached.' The next day the nurse called again: 'We've got salmon or chicken and we give it to the dogs by hand: which do you think your Safi would prefer?'

Safi made it home. He even beat the odds and lasted just beyond the promised year. Mitzpah's arrival definitely helped him. The advent of a young, undisciplined puppy gave him a new purpose in life, someone to boss around and attempt to bring into line. He only complained if we showed such lack of deference for his age as to feed the young upstart first, or if the latter dared to steal his food, or if, in his youthful enthusiasm, Mitzpah inadvertently knocked him over. I wondered if Safi understood that this was to be his successor in our home when he was gone, and what he might feel about it.

That summer, when we took him to Scotland, Safi slipped off the platform at Euston while we were walking along the sleeper train to find our carriage. Mercifully, Nicky managed to pull him back up. For a long time, I'd been watching with a growing sense of anguish how his step was becoming less even, his limp more pronounced. He'd been on a daily dose of Metacam for several seasons to ease his deteriorating joints. For years, I had feared the swift passing of his days, and watched – with an unease that grew into dread – the deterioration of his gait.

Safi's last Highland walk was on the island of Raasay. 'Let him come; he wants to go with us,' Nicky insisted, rightly. I had been minded to leave him behind in the cool of the shady car, fearing the steep woodland walk would be a torment to him. And he came, and even ran a little, and lolloped along, and loved his breaths of sea and mountain air.

Then, one freezing November night back home in London, he went out into the garden and disappeared. He wasn't on the lawn where I usually found him, or among the flowerbeds either. I took a torch and began to search, discovering him shivering down in the pond, unable to clamber back up. It wasn't clear whether he'd fallen in, or chosen to climb into the water in the hope of relieving the weight on his arthritic limbs. I called Nicky to help me; we lifted him out, bathed him, dried him off gently, gave him warm milk to drink and settled him back down. But we both understood: we couldn't, we shouldn't let this continue. What if he were to drown in his own back garden?

We didn't want to have to make the decision. Even when it's an animal, few people want to play God and take responsibility for what most of us would prefer to let destiny or the deity decide.

We spoke to each of the children. I asked my mother: 'Had the time now come? Was this the right thing to do? Were we sure? None of us was able to deny the inevitability of the conclusion. We wept, but were agreed. We made the feared appointment.

The children took Safi for a last walk, a slow meander round his favourite trees outside our house. We told them they could feed him any treat they pleased, even chocolate.

We decided to leave Mitzpah at home; it was fitting neither for Safi nor for him that this should be something he witnessed. Nicky reminded me when I was writing this book that, even though we had driven to the vet dozens of times, on this occasion we succeeded in getting ourselves lost. Somehow, I'd managed to let all recollection of this Freudian error disappear from my memory.

Our wise and gentle vet Geoffrey opened the surgery specially; there was no one else there that late evening to intrude on our farewells when we lifted Safi onto the table for the last time. We prayed with him, because every individual life is part of the sacred bond of all life. I carefully put my hand over his eyes, as is the custom to avoid distraction when reciting the Shéma meditation, in which the oneness of God in all things is proclaimed. Then Geoffrey gave Safi the injections, gently helping him to his place in the world to come. I felt the dog grow still and lie without life in my hands.

In the morning, I stared at Safi's untouched water bowl, his lead lying on the hall table, his dog towels, the half-used bottle of Metacam.

We buried Safi's ashes by the garden path in front of the house, so that we would think of him in all our comings and goings. We planted a dogwood tree on the spot; we would see the young leaves in spring, the flowers in late May and the burning red foliage in autumn. We set snowdrops underneath it, to mark the place with grace in winter too, because he was always a beautiful, faithful, kind and loving dog.

From time to time I still take down one or other of the photograph albums, which Nicky has carefully put together to help us remember and be thankful for all the wonderful years we've had together as a family, and which now fill three long shelves. I look for the pictures of Safi when he has just come to our house, when we first take him to Scotland, when we set out together on our mud-loving walks through the wintery bogs of the New Forest, when he's swinging and singing from the ropes on which he so loved to play.

I still sometimes crawl into a corner when I'm alone in the house and think of the years with Safi. Then I call to Mitzpah and even he, not a licking sort of dog, makes to lick my face. Then he rolls over and taps me with his paw to get me to tickle his tummy in his well-versed strategy of affectionate diversion.

We received tens of replies when I wrote in my weekly letter to my congregation that our beloved dog had died. It's often said that anyone who doesn't have a pet of their own simply doesn't get it, but most people really did seem to understand:

We imagine he was a companion and counsellor in times of stress whom you will greatly miss. *Bernard and Barbara Jackson*

I always remember dear Safi by your side . . . a shadow following humbly in your footsteps. To misquote Psalm 121, 'Safi was your shadow at your right hand.' *David Jackson*

I certainly believe dogs share the same amount of God's spirit as I do. Our intellects are different, but how anyone can believe that animals have no souls completely escapes me. So I assume that they find their rest under the wings of the Shechinah, the divine presence, just as we do – whether as ourselves or as part of the soul of Life I have no idea . . . I am crying as I write this, missing people and dogs rather badly. *Roberta Harris Eckstein*

The loss of Safi hurt, slowly and over a long time. It would have been far harder if we hadn't had Mitzpah to console us. It wasn't as devastating for us as it was for the friends who eventually explained why they wouldn't allow our animals into their home: 'You see, we've never gotten over the grief of losing our beloved retriever and we can't face the sight of another dog in the house.'

I once overheard a phone conversation in which the girl at my end of the line was trying to comfort a bereaved friend: 'You must be so upset . . . It's so terribly sad . . . You must miss her so much,' she kept saying at uneven intervals, during which her interlocutor was no doubt telling her how utterly grief-stricken he felt. I assumed her companion must recently have been widowed. It was only when she said, 'Why don't you go and get another one?' that I realised the subject in question had to be a dog.

But for all I know, the man at the far end of the line might have found that comment profoundly hurtful. A friend who desperately missed her dog said to me recently, 'You'd never think of telling a bereaved parent to go and have another baby, would you? Well, that's how hurt and insulted I feel when people say, "Just go to the rescue centre and pick up a new puppy!"' Sadly, she's not entirely correct; I know of grief-stricken parents who've been told exactly that: that it'll all be OK because 'they can have another baby, can't they', and they're presumably supposed simply to forget that unfortunate stillborn 'thing'.

The loss of every life by which we've been deeply touched stays with us always. Alongside the love, the sorrow, too, becomes part of our soul; though, hopefully, it is the love which is pre-eminent. That, to me, is the best answer to the question, 'Where is he now?' Of course, there are those who are sure their dogs are waiting for them in heaven. 'Paradise is open to all of God's creatures,' Pope Francis was said to have told a young, grieving boy who had just lost his dog.

I, too, can't imagine heaven, if heaven really is a physical abode, in which dogs are not there. If God is love, and present in all the love there is, then surely dogs must belong with God, and where else is that but heaven?

Victoria Gardner, for many years a dog trainer before she also became a psychologist and spiritual mentor, wrote in *BellaSpark* magazine of how 'once a dog bonds to a human, its soul attaches to the human's soul and, upon death, goes where the human soul goes. Indeed, thousands of people who have had a near death experience report being greeted in the next life by their beloved pets who have already crossed.'

I'm not sure what I think of so explicit a description of what happens in that 'undiscovered country from whose bourn no traveller returned', as Shakespeare's Hamlet describes it. Instead, I try to imagine that eternal present about which I heard a bereaved mother speak many years ago at Great Ormond Street Hospital: 'My child is outside of time now, so time can't take him further away. I think of him near me, as he once was, and that nothing has the power to separate us further.'

But it's not the dog's soul most of us are sad about, it's the huge physical and emotional void where that bounding, loving animal used to be. A poem found widely on the Internet and partially reprinted in the newsletter of the Cinnamon Trust describes the absence well, even while trying to offer the reassurance that our deeply adored dog really is still with us all the while:

Grieving

. . . I was with you at my grave today
You tend it with such care
I want to reassure you
That I'm not lying there.

I walked with you towards the house
As you fumbled for your key
I gently put my paw on you
I smiled and said it's me.

You looked so very tired
As you sank into your chair
I've tried so hard to let you know
That I was standing there . . .

Paradoxically, the poem leaves the impression that, for all the dog's faithful efforts, the weary, grief-stricken owner is unable to perceive him. As Shakespeare's King Lear said, 'I know when one is dead and when one lives', and there's no confusing the boundaries between the worlds.

Now it's the steady progression of Mitzpah's passing years which I dread. I observe him with tender but acute affection: if only I could make him into a puppy again! But then, he was such a rascal when he was small, so seemingly unbiddable that I sometimes wondered if we would ever manage to tame him. 'He sleeps a lot now-adays,' the children comment, looking at him on the old sofa in the kitchen, his head on a pillow, his eyes closed. 'He's getting old,' I say; then, swiftly turning my thoughts away from that direction which I so much fear, I add, 'But he's had two good walks today and he still loves to run.' And run he does when I take him at night onto the green and throw him sticks and say my prayers, for his life and mine, and for everything that lives.

Conclusion

Without the dogs, I wouldn't have blessed each tail-wagging morning with the same 'carpe canem' joy

He's looking at you with so much love,' a friend observes as Mitzpah stares up at us from underneath the table.

'It's mutual,' I say, and afterwards feel a fool for being so sentimental. But without the dog my heart would be less open, not just to animals but to people, nature, the presence of God in the world.

The Hebrew for dog is *kelev*. Taken on its own, the second syllable '*lev*' means 'heart'. When '*ke*' precedes a word, it signifies a comparison, 'like'. So *ke-lev* can also mean 'like the heart'; a dog is like the heart. My dogs have not just helped me discover more of my own heart, and the hearts of others; they have led me deeper into the heart of what matters most in life: trust, generosity and a listening, receptive soul.

Without the dogs, Nicky and I wouldn't have gone out at four o'clock one May morning in Wales when Safi was old and Mitzpah so young he'd woken us by messing on the floor; and, after cleaning up, we'd put on our boots and taken the puppy and watched the dawn transform the steep dark fields into sparkling green, and listened to the birds and the calls of the lambs, and returned an hour later refreshed and rejoicing because life itself had blessed us, and gone back to sleep with the dogs at rest on the floor.

Without those dogs, I wouldn't have reached wearily for my anorak at quarter to midnight and headed through the early autumn cold for the heath, where, releasing Mitzpah from the lead, I would watch my tiredness evaporate like the mist from my breath, and feel, as I followed at a run the dog's disappearing tail, what a joy it was to be alive; and, stopping to watch a hedgehog crawl through the grass, and inhaling the sharp air beneath the trees, understood how deeply vibrant all this living world is.

Without the dogs, I wouldn't have been so aware of the frightening swiftness of the passage of time. I wouldn't have observed with an anxious heart how,

Conclusion

summer by summer, Safi's hips were getting weaker, or felt with such fear the steady, irreversible encroachment of mortality on the puppy-young boisterousness of our companionship. I wouldn't have been marked so intensely, watching the dog years flow irreversibly through the hourglass, or been rendered so vulnerable, by the irretrievable preciousness of the days. I wouldn't have blessed each tail-wagging morning with the same *carpe canem* joy.

I've measured out my life by the way the dog runs, tugs, walks, begins to limp, becomes more pronouncedly halt. Is this his final summer? Our last summer together? I see Mitzpah and the children playing on Gairloch Beach in the last red glimmer of the western twilight across the blackening water. I watch them slowly turn into shadows, moving in the gentle tide, fading with everything visible into the all-embracing dark, and turn away and weep.

And I know, I must not waste it: this fragile gift of fleeting time for wonder, companionship and love.

References

Websites of organisations

All Dogs Matter: Dog rescue and rehoming in London
http://alldogsmatter.co.uk/

Battersea Dogs and Cats Home https://www.battersea.org.uk/

The Blue Cross: Helping sick, homeless and injured pets
https://www.bluecross.org.uk/

Brooke: Action for Working Horses and Donkeys
https://www.thebrooke.org/our-work

Canine Partners: Amazing Dogs Transforming Lives
https://caninepartners.org.uk/

The Cinnamon Trust: The National Charity for the
elderly, the terminally ill and their pets
http://www.cinnamon.org.uk/

The Dogs Trust: Bringing about the day when all dogs
can enjoy a happy life https://www.dogstrust.org.uk/

Guide Dogs for Blind People: http://www.guidedogs.org.uk/

Medical Detection Dogs, including Medical Alert Dogs: Training dogs to detect human disease https://www. medicaldetectiondogs.org.uk/

Pup Aid: Raising awareness of the horrific practice of puppy farming
http://pupaid.org/

The Royal Society for the Protection of Animals https:// www.rspca.org.uk/home

The Tanzie Project: supporting the forgotten pets of Boznia, Herzegovina and the Balkans http://www. thetanzieproject.org/

Books

Alexievich, Svetlana: *Chernobyl Prayer*, trans. Anna Gunin and Arch Tait (Penguin Books, 2016)

Bulanda, Susan (ed.): *Faithful Friends*: Holocaust Survivors' Stories of their Pets (Cladach Publishing, 2011)

Guest, Claire: *Daisy's Gift*: The remarkable cancer-detecting dog who saved my life (Virgin books, 2016)

Horowitz, Alexandra: *Inside Of A Dog*, What Dogs See, Smell and Know (Simon & Schuster, 2010)

Jennings, Linda: *Buster*, illustrated by Catherine Walters (Magi Publications, 1993)

References

O'Hanlon, Eleanor: *Eyes of the Wild*: Journeys of Transformation with the Animal Powers (Earth Books, 2012)

Oliver, Mary: *Dog Songs* (The Penguin Press, 2013)

Wild, Karen: *Being A Dog*: The world from your dog's point of view (Hamlyn, 2016)

Do you wish this wasn't the end?

Join us at www.hodder.co.uk, or follow us on
Twitter @hodderbooks to be a part of our community
of people who love the very best in books and reading.

Whether you want to discover more about a book
or an author, watch trailers and interviews, have the
chance to win early limited editions, or simply browse
our expert readers' selection of the very best books,
we think you'll find what you're looking for.

And if you don't,
that's the place to tell us what's missing.

We love what we do, and we'd love you to be part of it.

www.hodder.co.uk

@hodderbooks

HodderBooks

HodderBooks